NOF

M000073567

BACK ROADS

of
NORTHERN ALBERTA

by
JOAN DONALDSON-YARMEY

LONE
PINE

Dedicated to my family members who gave their total support and encouragement. I love you all for that. To Chevy, my four-legged travelling companion.

The publisher:
Lone Pine Publishing
206, 10426-81 Avenue
Edmonton, Alberta, Canada
T6E 1X5

Canadian Cataloguing in Publication Data

Donaldson-Yarmey, Joan, 1949
  Backroads of northern Alberta

  Includes bibliographical references and index.
  ISBN 0-919433-97-9

  1. Alberta — Guidebooks.   2. Rural roads — Alberta — Guidebooks.   I. Title.
FC3657.D65 1992   917.123'1043   C92-091571-x
F1076.D65 1992

Front cover photo: *Daryl Benson*
Cover and layout design: *Beata Kurpinski*
Illustrations: *Doris Chaput*
Photography: *Joan Donaldson - Yarmey*
Maps: *Gary Whyte, Phillip Kennedy*
Editorial: *Tanya Stewart, Lloyd Dick, Phillip Kennedy*
Printing: *Best Gagné Book Manufacturers Inc.*

The publisher gratefully acknowledges the assistance of the Federal Department of
Communications, Alberta Culture and Multiculturalism, and the Alberta Foundation for the
Arts in the production of this book.

Contents

Acknowledgements

In researching and updating material for this book, I travelled over 13,000 kilometres (8,190 miles), covering all the paved and most of the gravelled roads of northern Alberta. I interviewed many people, in person and over the telephone, spent months reading newspapers, magazines, brochures, and books, and visited all the sites, both natural and man-made.

When I did my updating, I discovered that the province is in a constant state of change — new attractions had appeared, different roads had been constructed into some sites, while other sites had been upgraded, new craft shops had opened and a few had closed. I hope any changes since the publication of this book will only add to the adventure.

Many thanks go to the friendly people of Alberta who took the time to answer my questions, gave me directions or personally took me to hard-to-reach sites, and sent me information. Without you, this book wouldn't have been possible.

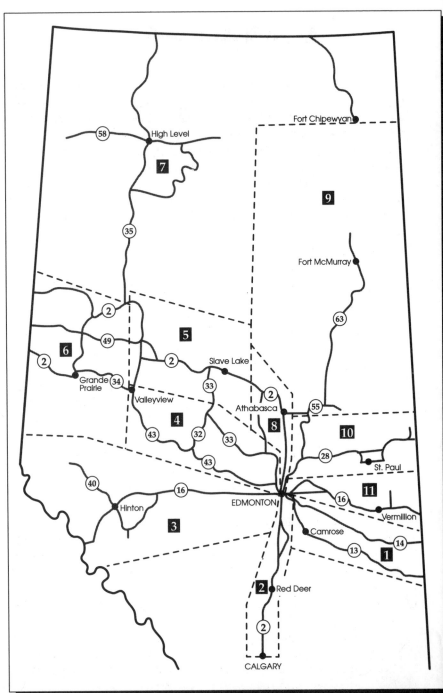

Introduction

Many people, tourist and resident alike, think of Alberta in terms of mountains, Lake Louise, Banff, Jasper, the Calgary Stampede, and West Edmonton Mall. Once they have seen those sights, they head off to "more exciting" distant lands. Very few take the time to pause and see the "other" Alberta.

Alberta roads offer something for every visitor. Besides the traditional museums and historical buildings, you will find antique shops, arts and crafts shops, golf courses, ski hills, cross-country skiing trails, thousands of lakes, rivers, and streams, small and big game, waterfowl, upland birds, and the most beautiful and varied scenery for photographers and artists.

Wildlife abounds along Alberta highways. Hawks soar overhead or, on a hot day, sit on fence posts with their wings hanging down, cooling themselves. There is hardly a road that doesn't have gophers watching the traffic from the sidelines. Occasionally, deer, moose, or other large animals lope across the highway. The chatter of squirrels and the singing of birds is heard at every campsite.

With some 3,000 campgrounds and thousands of hotels and motels throughout the province, visitors should have no worries about finding accommodations for the night.

Many towns have regularly scheduled activities throughout the year including rodeos, fairs, exhibitions, and farmers' markets. Striving to keep their communities beautiful, some have painted murals on the outside walls of stores and cartoon figures or little people on their fire hydrants.

The "Princess Province" has five distinct ecological zones: grassland, aspen parkland, foothills, mountains, and boreal forest. The only landscape missing is an ocean. Not only does each zone have its own plants, insects, birds, and animals, but each also has some that are rare, unusual, and surprising.

Backroads of Northern Alberta in no way pretends to cover all that there is to see and do in this part of the province. It is designed to give you an awareness of some of the famous and infamous citizens, the natural and man-made attractions, the stories and the humour of the hamlets, villages, towns, and cities of the rest of Alberta, and to get you started on your own explorations and discoveries. It is divided into sections covering roads that share the same history or the same scenery, are in the same ecological zone, or make a nice one-day trip.

It was impossible to include all the towns on all the backroads of northern Alberta in this book, so apologies are extended to the ones missed. But just because they are not in the book does not mean the reader should pass them by. Each has its own story, or history, or site to see.

So don't hurry through our province. Stay and enjoy. And remember — many of these sights can only be seen in Alberta.

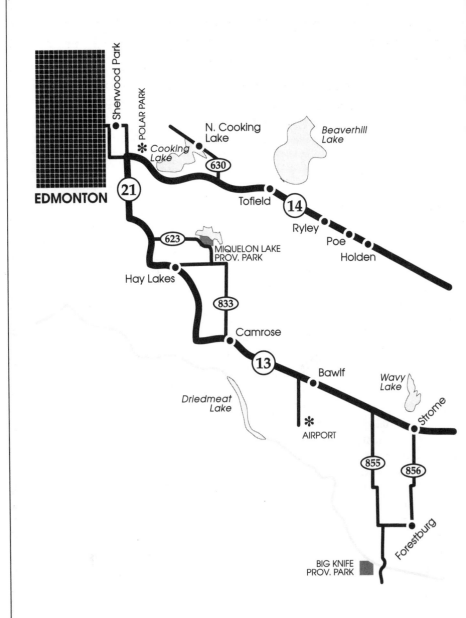

Chapter 1
Hardisty to Wainwright

This circuit is completely within Alberta's aspen parkland zone. You can expect to see some beautiful landscape, especially as you drive through the hills along the Battle River.

The Iron Creek Meteorite, the largest meteorite found to date in Canada, was discovered northeast of Killam by Reverend George McDougall in 1869. The meteorite is about 1,000 years old and weighs 165 kilograms (363 ponds). It was delivered to a museum in Toronto shortly after its discovery, but is now in the Provincial Museum of Alberta in Edmonton.

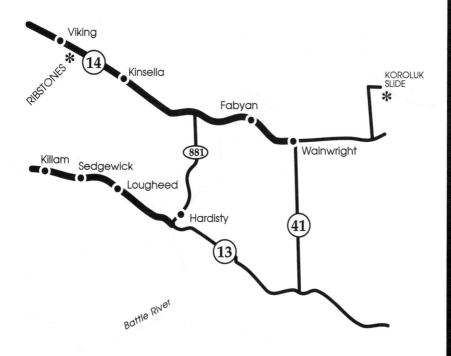

Hardisty to Bawlf

Hardisty is known as "Flag Capital of The World." A Flag Society was formed in the town a few years ago, and it received hundreds of banners and many messages from world leaders that encouraged tolerance, understanding, and brotherhood throughout the world. The flags hung in various sections of town until the society disbanded.

Flags at Hardisty Rodeo Grounds

Now, the only time you will see these flags flying is during the Hardisty Rodeo, when they are positioned around the rodeo grounds. Some of them are also on display at the Town office. At the Park of Provinces, you can see flags from across Canada and read the messages from the Prime Minister, the provincial premiers, and the territorial administrators.

During the rodeo, stay at the Hardisty Lake Park across from the grounds. The lake is a lovely blue and great for waterskiing, swimming, and boating. Fishermen will be pleased to know it is stocked with trout.

In the fall, hunters might want to try for whitetail and mule deer in the area.

LOUGHEED, SEDGEWICK, AND KILLAM

Lougheed was named after Senator Sir James Lougheed, former Premier Peter Lougheed's grandfather. For a look at the shoemaker's trade, visit the Iron Creek Museum in the village. You will see stitching machines, tools, old shoes, and samples of leather used by the shoemaker of a by-gone era.

Sedgewick won second prize in a "Best Water in Western Canada" competition. Their water source is only 5.5 metres (18 feet) below ground level.

The Iron Creek Meteorite, the largest meteorite found to date in Canada, was discovered northeast of Killam by Reverend George McDougall in 1869. The meteorite is about 1,000 years old and weighs 165 kilograms (363 pounds). It was delivered to a museum in Toronto shortly after its discovery, but is now in the Provincial Museum of Alberta in Edmonton.

The Sterling Flour Mills were constructed in Strome in 1911 and, over the years, gained a reputation for their modern equipment, model facilities, and superior quality products. Flour from here was shipped to central and northern Alberta and Saskatchewan. Flour was in great demand during the First World War, but the need decreased after the war and the mill closed in 1920. Twelve years later, it reopened and ran on a limited basis until 1942, when production was increased due to the Second World War. After years of operating at partial capacity, it finally shut its doors in 1963.

The faded white buildings still stand in Strome and the machinery inside is in good condition. Maybe one day the site will be restored to show visitors how a flour mill operated.

Quicksilver Manufacturing is located in Strome. They fabricate fibreglass canoes and export them throughout North America. Take a tour of the plant and have a cup of coffee, on the company.

North of Strome is Wavy Lake, a favorite layover for geese and ducks on their migrations.

FORESTBURG

Forestburg is south of Strome on #856. In 1907, adventurous homesteaders from the area began developing drift mines, also known as "gopher hole" mines, in the seams of coal along the banks of the Battle River. The coal was extracted by hand and loaded into coal cars, which were hauled to the surface by hand or by horse power. As many as 25 mines operated in the area, and most of these were owned by local residents. The Bish brothers owned one of the largest and their 25 employees produced 8,000 tonnes (8,889 tons) annually.

Coal Mine Cart, Devonian Park, Forestburg

These underground mines produced coal until 1949, when the Sinclair Coal Company bought out the Battle River Syndicate, which had been formed by some of the coal owners. The name Forestburg Collieries was given to the operation, and surface mining was begun in the area in 1950. In 1956, the collieries were sold to the Luscar mining group.

In the Devonian Park, you will see a coal mine car, typical of those used in the underground mines in the area from 1905 to 1945. At the entrance to the park is a cairn to commemorate Forestburg's becoming a village in 1919. Also on the monument is a plaque to Anthony Henday who camped west of the village on Oct. 4, 1754 during his exploration of the West.

Anthony Henday

In 1754, Anthony Henday became the first European to enter what is now Alberta, north of where Chauvin is today. He was employed by the Hudson's Bay Company and his mission was to convince the Blackfoot to make the four month round trip voyage to the Hudson's Bay to trade their furs. • With his Cree guides, he journeyed west and camped for three days in the valley of the Battle River. Like the Cree, Henday travelled on foot. When he reached an Assiniboine camp near present-day Irma, he bartered a gun for a horse, and so became Alberta's first white horse trader. • Henday was used to the grimy, disordered state of Cree camps, and wasn't prepared for the grandeur of the Blackfoot encampment. Two hundred teepees were assembled in two rows almost a mile long, and the Chief's tent could accommodate 50 people. • After smoking grand-pipes and eating boiled buffalo meat, Henday made his proposal. The Blackfoot Chief turned down Henday's request, politely pointing out that it was a great distance and they were not paddlers. Undaunted, Henday tried again the next day. Once more, his suggestion was rejected. • Henday and his Cree companions left the Blackfoot and, travelling west, crossed the Red Deer River near Innisfail, where Henday became the first European to view the Rocky Mountains. They camped for the winter along the North Saskatchewan River near the mouth of the Sturgeon River, north of present-day Edmonton. • Henday and the Cree returned to York Factory on Hudson's Bay with 60 canoes laden with Blackfoot furs. The Blackfoot had actually been trading their furs to the Cree, who had claimed them as their own when they reached the Bay. Not wanting to waste their time travelling to trade furs, the Blackfoot had refused to change their lifestyle.

The scenery along the Battle River valley at Big Knife Provincial Park, nine kilometres (5.5 miles) south of Forestburg on #855, is superb. To take some great photographs of the many channels the river has cut, climb the hill on the north side of the roadway into the park. Be careful where you step — the hill is covered with bright-yellow-flowered, prickly pear cacti.

Big Knife Provincial Park

Forestburg Collieries at Paintearth Mine is twenty kilometres (12 miles) south of Forestburg on Highway #856 and one kilometre (0.6 miles) east on #601. Drive slowly along #601 and read the signs posted in the fields. These explain what was mined out, when the land was levelled, the date the soil was replaced, and when and what was seeded. Stop in at the office, Monday to Friday during office hours, for a tour or phone (403) 582-4112 for information.

Mining Equipment

When the Diplomat Mine opened in 1950, second hand equipment was brought up from the United States for the operation. One such piece was the Marion 360 — the world's largest mobile land machine at the time of its construction in 1923. It had originally been a dragline but was converted to a stripping shovel in 1950. As a shovel, it stripped the surface ground from the coal seams at the Diplomat mine and deposited it in a mined-out cut. It was first retired in 1962, then brought out in 1975 to work another five years. • The Marion 360 was constructed before welding was widely used and was put together entirely with rivets. It still stands at the now unused Diplomat mine and is the only remaining machine of its type in the world. • As the demand for coal increased, new and larger stripping shovels and booms were erected. In 1962, the Bucyrus-Erie 950-B stripping shovel, with a 23 cubic metre (30 cubic yards) dipper on a 33 metre (107 foot) boom and weighing an incredible 1,200 tonnes (1,333 tons) was moved onto the site. It was Canada's largest shovel at the time and worked until the mine closed.

BAWLF

The Lutheran Church in Bawlf is the third one to be constructed in the village. When the first one was destroyed by fire, the members of the congregation built a second one. When it, too, burned, they erected this last one: made of brick.

Alberta's Littlest Airport is four kilometres (2.5 miles) west of Bawlf and four kilometres south on Kelsey Road. The airport is located in a farmer's field, and various groups use it for wiener roasts, corn roasts, and fun days. Avid remote control pilots gather in the evenings to practice on the five runways for the owner-sponsored flying competition in August.

Camrose to Tofield

CAMROSE

Camrose is a very easy town to explore. Obtain a map at the Chamber of Commerce and begin your visit. As you near the vicinity of an attraction, watch for "City tour" street signs with an arrow and number. Industrial tours through the Stelco Pipe Mills and the Byers Flour Mill, home of Sunny Boy Cereals, are also available.

Rosehaven and the Camrose Museum are both on 53rd Street, between 46th and 47th Avenues. Constructed in 1912, the

Miquelon Lake Provincial Park

building housing Rosehaven was initially called the Camrose Normal School. It was the second school opened in Alberta for the education of teachers. When the University of Alberta began offering classes for would-be instructors, this school suspended operation. A new wing was added, the grounds were landscaped, and now it is a hospital called Rosehaven.

Camrose Lutheran College is renowned for its Viking Cup hockey tournament, which attracts teams from Canada, the United States, and Europe. The college is also a Nordic skiing training centre. One of Canada's oldest ski clubs is in Camrose, and the runs are used by skiers hoping to qualify for provincial and national championships.

If you happen to be in town during the first weekend in June, you can take part in the annual Jaywalkers Jamboree. It features the CFCW Chicken Races and the Great Canadian Chili-Cook Off.

The Camrose Golf course is in Victoria Park, in the northwest corner of town. About two kilometres (1.2 miles) north of Camrose, on #833, is the Whistle Stop Driving Range and Miniature Golf Course.

There are northern pike in Dried Meat Lake to the south of town, and each winter an ice fishing derby is held at the lake.

For those looking for a place to camp for the night, continue north on #833 to Miquelon Lake

Miquelon Lake Provincial Park

Provincial Park. It has 286 camping sites and long, wide, sandy beaches on a large lake. The warm water is great for swimming, sailing, boating, windsurfing, and waterskiing. There is a 9-hole golf course, a petting zoo, go-karts, and mini-golf at Miquelon Funland. You should be able to find something to do, unless you are a fisherman — no angling is allowed.

HAY LAKES

Hay Lakes is Southwest of Miquelon, on Highway #617, and just east of the town is a campground. Walk through the gate at the south end and follow the road to a large open field. There is a slight hill in the centre of the field with a monument and three flag poles. This is the site of the most westerly telegraph station on the Battleford line, established in 1877. However, the station only operated two years. When the telegraph was extended from Battleford to Fort Edmonton in 1879, this office was abandoned.

Telegraph

When Canada acquired the Northwest Territories from the Hudson's Bay Company in 1869, there was a desperate need for a communication system. Finally, in 1874, the federal government employed private contractors to build an electric telegraph line along a proposed Canadian Pacific Railway route. The line was put up between 1874-78 and ran between Fort William, north of Winnipeg, and Hay Lakes. This united Eastern Canada with the West. • There were numerous complaints about the length of time it took for messages to reach the population of the NWT. There were many reasons for slow service: inadequate poles that were sometimes held up by the wire; occasional sections were supported by tree limbs; poor maintenance of the line; undersized poles; green wooden brackets that dried and eventually fell off; insufficient slack for contraction during cold weather; prairie fires; and lightning strikes. • In 1879, the line was rerouted from Battleford, through Victoria Settlement and Fort Saskatchewan, to Fort Edmonton. At this time, the CPR boasted that it had the longest telegraph line, working on a continuous circuit, in North America.

COOKING LAKE

The Cooking Lake-Blackfoot Recreation, Wildlife, and Grazing Area is west of Sherwood Park and south of Elk Island National Park. One of the earliest steps in conservation occurred here in 1899, when Canada's first forest reserve, the Cooking Lake Forest Reserve, was established. Management of the holding was taken over by the Alberta government in 1930.

In 1948, local cattlemen organized the Blackfoot Grazing Association and leased the reserve for pasture. By the late 1970s, outdoor recreationists were using the sanctuary for their own pursuits. All these activities, along with natural gas production, created a problem. So, in order to look after the needs of the wildlife, cattle, gas producers, and humans, the Cooking Lake-Blackfoot Grazing, Wildlife and Provincial Recreation Area was launched. It is unequaled anywhere in Alberta.

The area is on 97 square kilometres (37 square miles) of wetlands, pastures, and forests. It is an island of wildlife in a sea of agricultural land. Coyote, elk, moose, and more than 200 varieties of birds occupy the reserve, along with the cattle.

There are four staging sites: two can be reached from Highway #14, one from Highway #16, and one from Range Road #210. Drive into the staging enclosure, park your vehicle, and you are free to hike, ride horses, cross country ski, snowshoe, and snowmobile. Enjoy yourself, but remember to respect the other users of the land.

POLAR PARK

Polar Park is the first park of its kind in Alberta. Its main purpose is to preserve and breed animals, many of which are endangered, from the colder climates of the world. As you pull into the parking lot, watch for a flock of Canada geese that circles the lot, lands, waddles around honking, then flies up and starts the procedure over again. When you climb out of your car, listen for the lonesome howl of the wolves. It will send a tingle down your spine.

Polar Park

The animals are kept outdoors, so the park is open year round. There are about 600 hectares (1,500 acres) of land in the sanctuary, and wide paths lead you to the various sections. The best time to view the animals is during their noon feeding, when they gather close to the fence. In the winter, there are more than 16 kilometres (10 miles) of cross-country ski trails which will take you through the park and out into the forest preserve.

TOFIELD

Knothole Woodcraft is on the main street of Tofield. Enter the shop and you will be treated to a view of some very original wood products, which owner Eva Loranger has hand-crafted. Jewellery boxes, made from the end pieces of fence posts, and wood carvings line shelves. Wood burning drawings and barbed wire plaques hang on the walls. Lamps with wooden bases, carved animals, and painted signs are just a few of her other creations.

Eva will take the time to visit with you. She will explain the various types of wood and how each gives a piece of work a distinct look. Much of the wood she uses — mesquite, oak, cedar, and pine — is collected on expeditions to the United States. She also buys wire at barbed wire shows in the States.

At the south end of main street is William Rowan Park, named after a famous Canadian ornithologist. At the park is a large collection of bird houses donated by various towns, businesses, and clubs throughout the area. Each one is different and has the name of the donor on it.

East of Tofield, on Highway #626 is the Beaverhill Lake Natural Area and Bird Sanctuary. The natural area was established to conserve and maintain the wildlife and wilderness around the lake.

A group of birding enthusiasts formed the Beaverhill Lake Bird Banding Station in 1983 to facilitate research on the birds of the lake and to provide training in field ornithology. The association was renamed the Beaverhill Bird Observatory in 1985 and has remained active in many projects.

Beaverhill Lake is one of two nationally sanctioned nature viewpoints, and is western Canada's only shore bird reserve. Over 250 species of birds have been identified at the lake and many of them are rare or endangered.

If you would like to see large migrations, or maybe spot a rare bird, visit Beaverhill Lake. In March, local nesting pairs of Canada Geese appear and signal that spring has arrived. Soon many other species begin to appear: red-tail hawks, bald eagles, harriers, peregrine falcons, pectoral sandpipers, and marbled godwits. By May, the lake is alive with thousands of waterfowl. Some continue north; some stay and nest.

Soon the woods, fields, and marshes are full of song-birds. Some of the rarer birds — the black-billed cuckoo, the red phalarope, or the sharp-tailed sparrow — might be seen by watchful birders.

Red-tail hawks

To reach the Beaverhill Bird Observatory, follow Highway #626 (Rowan's Route) east of town. About four kilometres (2.5 miles) farther is a side road that leads to Francis Point.

Continue past Francis Point for another four kilometres and turn north. There is a closed gate across the access; make sure you secure it after you have entered the field. Drive slowly; the path is two tracks wide and deep ruts occasionally cut across it.

At the end of the path is another gate. This one you cannot drive through. Park your vehicle here, open the gate or climb through the fence, and proceed on foot. The walk to the observatory is through tall foliage and low wetland on the western shore of Robert Lister (or A) Lake. Eventually the path heads west away from this lake and ends at the bird observatory on Beaverhill Lake.

The trail is long, so make sure you have good hiking shoes, plenty of mosquito repellent, and a sun hat. Don't forget your camera. Because of the distance and the "herds"' of mosquitoes, only ardent bird watchers will want to make this trip.

Ryley to Wainwright

RYLEY, POE, AND HOLDEN

The welcoming sign at Ryley states "Live the Life of Ryley."

Have you heard of the famous "Captain and Mrs. Compost"? Did you know they make their home in Ryley? They are two people who dress in costumes and enter in local parades as mascots for Canada's first community compost project.

The natural fertilizer venture was begun by the residents of Ryley and district and is endorsed by the Village Council and the Department of the Environment. All organic matter — potato peels, coffee grounds, grass cuttings, anything originally taken from the ground — can be composted.

The villagers deliver their organic matter to a compound near the town where it is stored and left to work. Then, as they need it, they return to pick up the fertilizer for their yards and gardens. Ninety-four per cent of the village participates in the project.

The hamlet of Poe was named after the famous master of detective and horror stories, Edgar Allan Poe.

Holden does not have a museum, but you are allowed to visit the Holy Ghost Ukrainian Catholic Church to see its kaleidoscopic interior.

VIKING

In 1914, gas was found in the area and Viking became the centre of the Viking Gas Field. Natural gas from this field has served Edmonton, Red Deer, and towns between since that initial find.

The Viking Meat Market and Processing Plant is the "Home of the Famous Viking Sausage." The sausage is long and slim, like a pepperoni, although lighter in colour and not as wrinkled. It has a mild taste. It is sometimes called a wiener and you can munch on it while you travel.

Ribstone near Viking

The town is also the "Home of the Sutters," a family that had six brothers who played in the NHL at the same time.

To see the Viking Ribstones, watch for an historical sign about 11 kilometres (seven miles) east of the town. Just past that sign is a road heading south. Follow it until you come to a "T" intersection. Turn east and then immediately south again. There isn't a sign announcing the ribstones. Watch for the red and white fence posts surrounding a slight hill on the west side of the road. Drive to the top and you will find the ribstones and a cairn.

The large stones have carvings similar to the ribs of a buffalo. Scientists believe they were worshiped by Natives for many centuries. They left gifts of tobacco, beads, or meat beside the ribstones in the hopes that it would bring them luck during their hunt. This custom was continued until the late 1800s. Because they are of historic value, please do not disturb them.

KINSELLA AND FABYAN

Kinsella has a large building, divided into three businesses, along the highway. One is the Kinsella Kountry Store, another is the Kinsella Kountry Kafe, and the third is the Kinsella Kountry Post Office. The first log cabin in this hamlet, built in 1903, is used as a small museum.

If you are an antique lover, stop in at Antiques by Herrod in Fabyan. It is located, appropriately, in a church built in 1911, and is on the west corner as you turn off the highway. The owner operated an antique shop in Scotland for many years before moving back to Alberta, and most of the articles come from that country.

WAINWRIGHT

Camp Wainwright is Canada's second largest military training facility and western Canada's main training base. During the war, over 1,000 German officers were interred at the camp. A P.O.W. tower, with artifacts, commemorates that time. If you ask at the gate to see the tower, you will only be allowed to drive

POW Tower, Camp Wainwright

up to it and take pictures. A tour of the inside can be arranged at the Wainwright tourist booth.

Beside the camp is a paddock containing a small herd of buffalo. A narrow road follows the fence and there are many turnouts, called "Buffalo Lookout Parking," which hold about three vehicles. The best time to see these huge animals is in the evening when they come out of the bush for water and salt.

Canada's largest falcon facility is in Wainwright. Endangered Peregrine falcons are raised here and released into the wild. To view the Peregrine Falcon Facility, you must book a tour at the tourist information booth, because the road to the complex is through Camp Wainwright.

Buffalo National Park

Before Camp Wainwright was established, the area was known as Buffalo National Park. The park was created in 1908 on 592 square kilometres (234 square miles), and buffalo, elk, and moose roamed throughout its forests. In 1941, the buffalo were transferred to Elk Island National Park and the Department of National Defence took over the land.

Petroleum Park is on the same grounds as the tourist information booth. One of the first wooden oil pumps used in the area is on display. There is also an exhibit explaining the history of the petroleum industry in Wainwright.

About 20 kilometres (12 miles) east of Wainwright, on Highway #14, is the turn to the Koroluk Slide. The route is gravel, and you will pass the United Church of Rosedale, built in 1933. Continue for 22 kilometres (13.6 miles), then turn east at the "T" and drive to the slide.

The Koroluk slide occurred in 1974 and was caused when the subsoil strata (the layer of earth just under the ground surface) became saturated with water and very slippery. The heavy topsoil squeezed the subsoil and the subsoil (still underneath the surface) slid down the slope until it found a spot where the topsoil was lighter. Some of the earth slid 230 metres (750 feet) before stopping.

While this was happening, the surface soil sank to replace the lost subsoil, some of it dropping 12 to 15 metres (40 to 50 feet). The crops, grass, and bushes growing on the topsoil were barely disturbed by the change in their location.

Walk through the gate into the field and take a look at the slide area and the fence hanging out over the fallen terrain. Be careful where you stand. Cracks are opening up in the ground close to the edge of the cliff.

Koroluk slide

Chapter 2
Devon to Crossfield

Highway #2 is a perfect example of a thoroughfare designed to bypass nearby small towns. It was constructed for members of the human race in a hurry to reach their destination. But for those who want to "see" this part of Alberta, travel down Highway #2A. Though it is narrow and mostly shoulder-less (some sections are being widened), this is where the sights are.

Stop in at Kilborn Antiques in Millet, to see grandfather clocks, rolltop desks, table and chair sets, dishes, and lamps.

You can't visit Wetaskiwin without stopping in at the Reynold's Alberta Museum, with its collection of antique cars, trucks, tractors, steam engines, fire engines, war artifacts, and airplanes.

Ponoka is well-known for its annual stampede, held on the July long weekend. During the summer, the Ponoka Stampede Museum is open in the tourist information booth.

Red Deer is famous for its parks structure. You can hike or bicycle all across the city on paths connecting the smaller parks of the Waskasoo Park system.

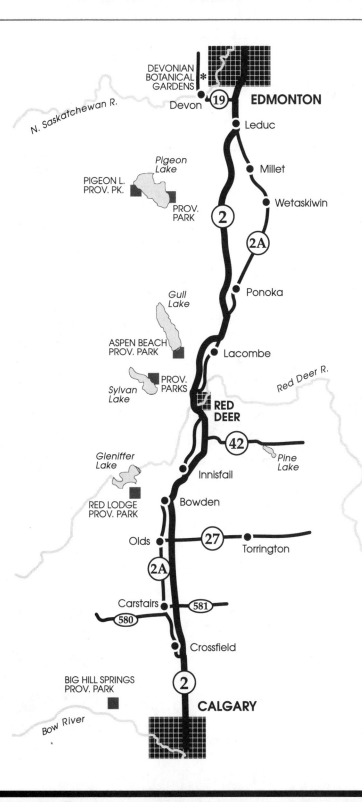

Devon to Lacombe

Devon is not located on #2A but is a good beginning for the drive. Oil was struck about one kilometre (0.6 miles) south of here in 1947, and this well was the start of the Leduc-Woodbend oil field. The new town that quickly sprang up was called Devon, after the Devonian rock formation base in which the oil was discovered. The Leduc Oil Field is now famous throughout the world.

On the site, one kilometre (0.6 miles) south of the town, is the Leduc #1 oil derrick, on the east side of Highway #60. The derrick is actually an antique similar to the original used to drill that Discovery well.

Native People's Garden, Devonian Botanic Gardens

Devon holds a raft race down the North Saskatchewan River in the summer. In the winter, the Nordic Ski Club operates a 55 metre (180 foot) and a 25 metre (80 foot) ski jump, for experts as well as beginners.

Drive five kilometres (three miles) north of Devon, through the North Saskatchewan River valley with its red banks and green trees, to the University of Alberta Devonian Botanic Gardens. Park in the large, flower-decorated lot and visit the gift shop for information before striking out on your tramp through the woods.

The gardens were developed by the University in 1959 and have several trails leading to many contrasting plant and animal communities. Some of the sections you will see are a five acre Japanese garden, a herb garden, a Native people's garden, desert plants, a peony collection, and woody ornamentals.

The walk is enjoyable, but remember that the garden is in a natural setting and has many of the hazards of a regular forest. Watch for wet ground, tree roots, and mosquitoes.

Japanese Garden, Devonian Botanic Gardens

LEDUC

Drive south of Devon on Highway #60 to Highway #39. Turn east and head for Leduc. Many of the towns of Alberta received their names from Catholic priests who served the communities. Leduc is one such town. When the postmaster opened his office, he wanted a name for it but had a hard time picking one. Finally,

Leduc #1 Well

one day he decided to name it after the first person who walked in the door. Father Leduc, who had walked many miles in the cold, stopped in at the office to warm up and the town's name was set.

In an effort to encourage the food preparation industry in the province, a food processing centre, sponsored by the Government of Alberta, was established in Leduc. Facilities, technical expertise, equipment, and financial help are available to food processors. At the centre, companies are able to fully analyze their proposed food preparation methods, before making any large investment.

MILLET

Stop in at Kilborn Antiques in Millet, to see grandfather clocks, rolltop desks, table and chair sets, dishes, and lamps. The owners travel all over Canada in search of antiques for their business. They have a personal glassware collection consisting of cutglass dating back to the early 1900s, dishes, and lamps from the 1880s. Occasionally, they display this collection at the Millet museum.

WETASKIWIN

The Legend of Wetaskiwin-Spatinow

One day, a war party of Blackfoot and a war party of Cree were unknowingly riding towards each other. That night they camped on opposite sides of a hill. A young chief from one band decided to scout the hill. At the top he met a chief from the other band and they immediately began wrestling. They struggled for many hours before pausing to rest. • The Blackfoot lit his pipe, but when the Cree went to light his, he found that it had been broken in the scuffle. The Blackfoot offered his; the Cree accepted and began puffing. They suddenly realized they had just smoked the pipe of peace. Each quickly returned to his camp and related the tale to the other members of the band. • Everyone felt it was a sign that peace should be made. Chiefs from both tribes assembled and passed the peace pipe from mouth to mouth. That hill became known as Wetaskiwin-Spatinow — "the hill where peace was made."

During the North West (Riel) Rebellion in 1885, the Alberta Field Force build Fort Ethier, a blockhouse on land owned by the Lucas family, five miles north of present-day Wetaskiwin. When the threat of war subsided, the fort was used as a stopover house on the Edmonton-Calgary trail.

The blockhouse still stands today. It is small but has two storeys — the ground floor about 1.2 metres (four feet) high and a top level, not much higher. The second storey has 12 loopholes through which soldiers could fire at the rebels. These defences proved unnecessary, as not one shot was discharged in the battle at the fort. You may obtain directions to the farm at the information booth in Wetaskiwin, but the blockhouse is on private land, so you should phone ahead if you want to visit.

Fort Ethier

You can't visit Wetaskiwin without stopping in at the Reynold's Alberta Museum, with its collection of antique cars, trucks, tractors, steam engines, fire engines, war artifacts, and airplanes. It was first opened to the public in 1955 under the name Reynold's Museum. Over the years, it has expanded and was finally moved to a new site, three minutes west of the city on Highway 13.

The oldest aircraft at the museum is a 1918 Curtiss JN4 Canuck. It was christened the "City of Edmonton" and was piloted by Wop May and George Gorman until 1924. Its last flight was in the 1930s.

Wetaskiwin isn't noted just for its vintage vehicles. The town has the highest per capita automotive sales in Canada and is known as the car capital of the country. Drive the "Automile" and maybe you can make a deal on a vehicle while you are in town.

PONOKA

Ponoka is well-known for its annual stampede, held on the July long weekend. During the summer, the Ponoka Stampede Museum is open in the tourist information booth. Saddles, a young Native woman in full dress, trophies, a chuck wagon, and many old photographs of the rodeo are on exhibit. Inhale deeply and savour the aroma of old leather blended with a trace of tanned hide.

Ponoka is also the home of the Fort Ostell Museum. Fort Ostell was one of the posts established by the Alberta Field Force during the North West (Riel) Rebellion. There are picnic tables set on a large lawn and a fishing pond at the museum.

Alberta Field Force

Before the actual uprising called the North West (Riel) Rebellion occurred in Saskatchewan in 1885, the native's and Métis' representative, a Métis named Louis Riel, sent a petition to Ottawa stating their grievances. Ignoring the petition, the government ordered the Canadian Militia, under Lieutenant-General F.D. Middleton, west to suppress any uprising that might occur. Ottawa also directed a telegram to retired Major-General Thomas Bland Strange at Gleichen requesting that he form an Alberta Field Force and stand by in case Middleton should need assistance. • General Strange headed to Calgary and began to assemble his force, first enlisting cowboys who were used to taking orders and skilled in riding and shooting. They became the Alberta Mounted Rifles under Major J. Hutton. Strange summoned NWMP Inspector Sam Steele from British Columbia to form a unit called Steele's Scouts. • On April 2, 1885, nine men, including two priests, were killed at Frog Lake by Chief Wandering Spirit, the War Chief of the Cree under Big Bear. After the massacre, the Plains Cree took four white men and women prisoner, looted and burned the buildings for a week, then headed for Fort Pitt in Saskatchewan accompanied by the Wood Crees and Chipewyans from Cold Lake. • General Strange was ordered to overtake Big Bear and free the prisoners, and on April 20, the Alberta Field Force began its pursuit of Big Bear. •General Strange divided the force into three groups. He commanded one, with Sam Steele under his charge. They were the first to leave Calgary. Major A. Bowen Perry was in charge of the second group and they quickly followed Strange. In order to foil any attempt by the natives to cut the army's communication lines, Major Perry left twenty men under Lieutenant Normandeau at the Red Deer Crossing with instructions to build a fort. They seized John McLellan's year-old hotel, reinforced it, installed loopholes, dug a moat, and called it Fort Normandeau. • As Perry and the remainder of his force travelled toward Edmonton, other posts were set up at the Battle River Crossing (Ponoka) and on Sam Lucas' farm near Pipestone Creek (Wetaskiwin). They were abandoned after the rebellion without a shot being fired in battle.

The Alberta Hospital at Ponoka has been in operation since 1911. It is a regional psychiatric treatment complex for central and southern Alberta. Throughout its history, it has worked to change the attitudes of society toward the mentally ill and to provide a high standard of patient care. It also is renowned for its training of psychiatric nurses.

LACOMBE

Lacombe was named after Father Albert Lacombe, a Roman Catholic missionary who spent his life working among the Native people. As part of its Mainstreet Project, the town has restored many of its historic buildings, some of which were

Michener House, Lacombe

constructed in the early 1900s. One of the more prominent structures is the Michener House where Daniel Roland Michener, Governor-General of Canada from 1967 to 1974, was born in 1900.

Roland Michener

Roland Michener graduated from the University of Alberta with the highest standing in the province, received a Rhodes Scholarship, and attended Hertford College in England, where he earned his law degree. He became involved in politics in the late 1930s and enjoyed a long life in the political field. He was elected to the House of Commons in 1953, was appointed High Commissioner to India in 1964 and Canadian Ambassador to Nepal in 1965, and was named Governor General in 1967. Always active in sports, he was known as "Canada's jogging Governor General." • The Alberta government named a mountain after him in 1979 (*Chapter 10*, Nordegg to Banff National Park section) and in 1982, at the age of 82, he climbed his mountain.

Red Deer and District

Red Deer is famous for its parks structure. You can hike or bicycle all across the city on paths connecting the smaller parks of the Waskasoo Park system. Each park has its own unique attractions.

At the Bower Ponds in Great Chief Park you can rent canoes, paddle boats, and fishing tackle. On the bank overlooking the ponds is Cronquist House. The three storey, 325 square metre (3500 square foot) Victorian structure was built in 1912.

Cronquist House, Red Deer

When Cronquist House was threatened with demolition in 1976, the Red Deer International Folk Festival Society decided to save it by relocating it. They stripped the bricks from the outside and removed the inside plaster. Then, while the Red Deer River was still frozen, they skidded it down the steep bank, across the ice, and up the other side to the Bower Ponds. Take a tour through the completely restored house, which is now a multicultural centre with exhibits, workshops, classes, a library, and a meeting room.

The Red Deer International Folk Festival is held on the July long weekend in the Great Chief Park. Many ethno-cultural groups from central Alberta gather for the celebration. Red Deer held its first folk festival in 1969.

Some of the other parks in the system are the Maskepetoon Athletic Park, the Rotary Park, the Great West Adventure Park, Heritage Ranch, and Fort Normandeau. The present Fort Normandeau is a replica, although some of the logs from the original were used in its construction. The fort is on the banks of the Red Deer River, west of Highway #2. It is linked to the other parks, first by river to Heritage Ranch, and then by trail to Great Chief Park.

Heritage Ranch offers trail, pony, and winter sleigh rides, and a viewing tower from which you can see the city centre and the Red Deer River.

Fort Normandeau

The walking tour of Red Deer covers 4.5 kilometres (2.8 miles) and takes you past more than 25 historical sites and buildings. In an effort to preserve the area's heritage while keeping up with modern times, the downtown Bank of Montreal set aside two corbels and a sandstone block from the original bank building, constructed in 1913. The corbels now hang on each side of the new entrance and the sandstone block lies in a flower bed in front of the doors.

One of Alberta's great architectural achievements is St. Mary's Church in Red Deer. It was designed by architect Douglas Cardinal and completed in 1968. The pattern was inspired by a spider's web. The exterior is flowing and semi-circular; the interior focuses on the altar with the aisles branching in different directions.

If downhill skiing is what you like, visit the Canyon Ski Area east of Red Deer on #595. This is the largest non-mountain ski resort in Alberta. It has two chairlifts, two T-bars, and

St. Mary's Church

a handle tow to get you up to the top. You then have a choice of 11 runs down the canyon of the Red Deer River.

Pine Lake, near Red Deer, is very popular with the residents of the area. To reach the lake, head south on Highway #2 to #42 and turn east. Follow the highway to Ghost Pine Trail and turn south. Resorts, a hotel, service stations, a dude ranch and campground, restaurant, store, day use only government campground, other campgrounds, and a trailer park are just some of the facilities at the lake. The Ghost Pine Lake Resort has the added feature of an indoor swimming pool. There is also a Salvation Army camp and a Prairie Bible Institute camp on the shores of the lake.

Ghost Pine Lake

According to legend, a party of Blackfoot massacred a camp of Cree on the shore of this lake in the early 1800s. One Cree warrior, who had been hunting, returned and found his family and friends dead. He painted his face black in mourning and began to stalk the Blackfoot. By entering their camp at night or attacking a lone brave, he was able to kill and scalp many enemies. The Blackfoot, thinking it was a ghost killing the braves, quickly fled the shores of what was thereafter known as Ghost Pine Lake or Devil's Pine Lake.

Innisfail to Crossfield

INNISFAIL

Innisfail was a popular layover on the Calgary to Edmonton trail in the 1880s. The only preserved stopping house from that era is in the historic village at Innisfail. The house was built in 1886 and was visited by stage coaches running the trail.

Innisfail also has the Hereford Breeding Test Centre. Based on 29 hectares (72 acres), it has the capacity to board up to 72 bulls at one time. The main objective of the centre is to improve the Hereford breed.

Innisfail Historical Village

Northwest of Innisfail is the high ground of Antler Ridge. It is from this ridge that Anthony Henday became the first European to see the Rocky Mountains.

BOWDEN

Between Innisfail and Bowden, Highways #2A and #2 merge into Highway #2. Before the town of Bowden, on the east side of the highway is the only RCMP dog training facility in Canada. Dogs are trained for most law enforcement agencies in the country and are taught obedience, agility, and criminal apprehension. Take a tour of the facility and view the instruction procedure.

If you like your fruit fresh and enjoy picking it, head west of Bowden on #587 to Pearson's U-pick Berry Farm. You can select your own strawberries in July, saskatoons from the end of July to the middle of August, and raspberries in August. There is also a limited supply of chokecherries, pincherries, currants, and hi-bush cranberries.

OLDS

Olds College has played an important role in Alberta's agricultural development since its opening in 1913. Tours of the campus and farm are available, and you will see rose gardens, landscaped lawns, and botanical green spaces. If you feel the need for exercise after hours of driving, the college's fitness centre is open to the public year round.

For hunters, Mountainview Taxidermy in Olds prepares life-size mounts of animals, birds in flight, fish, game heads, and the taxidermists will make rugs from skins and mount horns.

John Wayne's Convenience Store, Torrington

The A.H. Johnson ranch operates the Tack Corral in Olds, where you can buy new and used tack and saddles. For the first time horse owner, the ranch also holds clinics on green colt training, beginner jumping, and beginner riding, and has trail riding camps.

The Mountain View Handicapped Riding Association sponsors riding lessons for mentally and physically disabled people. The lessons are held from May to August on Tuesday and Thursday evenings at the Olds Cow Palace.

Did you know that John Wayne is alive and well and operating a store in Alberta? If you want to meet him, take Highway #27 east of Olds to Torrington. There you will find John Wayne's Convenience Store, with a large painting of a covered wagon above the door. Feel free to enter and visit with him, although he will be somewhat different from the man you remember from the movies.

John Wayne Johnson is his real moniker and his mother named him after the movie star. For the disappointed, there are a number of photographs of the actor John Wayne on the walls.

CARSTAIRS

Most towns have fairs and exhibitions—Carstairs has the Great Pumpkin Festival, in the last weekend of September. Growers for miles around spend their summers carefully cultivating

Atlantic Giants, hoping to receive first prize. The winning pumpkin the first year weighed 148 kilograms (326 pounds) and that record hasn't been broken.

Besides the pumpkin challenge, there is the King and Queen contest. Entrants have to draw the best pumpkin, carve a pumpkin, and outdo the others at pie eating. Another competition requires contestants to design an outfit for a pumpkin. The festivities end with a pioneer supper and dance.

Would you like to try your hand at growing and entering one of these great orange vegetables? There are three classes: Carstairs and area, the rest of the province, and outside the province. A pumpkin plumping tip: saturating the roots with milk is supposed to guarantee enormous growth.

Another attraction in Carstairs is its famous fudge. Stop in at the store on Main Street for a sample or purchase some from the booth at the Calgary Stampede.

A monument to Henry Wise Wood is on Hammond Street and 11th Avenue. Wood was a promoter of a strong farm organization and was president of the United Farmers' Association for 15 years.

Sheep

One of the oldest known domesticated animal is the sheep. Shepherds were guarding flocks against predators long before recorded history. Originally tamed for their hides and milk, and to carry burdens, sheep were carefully bred to replace their coarse hair with soft wool. This soft wool has been used for centuries in the making of material for clothing. • Alberta's sheep industry, with an annual production of over 567,000 kilograms (1 1/4 million pounds) of wool, is the most extensive in Canada.

Near Carstairs are two craft shops which make products from sheep wool. One, Pasu Farms, is southwest of Carstairs on #580; the other, Custom Woolen Mills is east on #581.

At Pasu Farms, the owners display weavings from Africa and sell tapestries, carvings, stuffed sheep toys, moccasins with sheep skin linings, hand knitted sweaters, mens' vests, coats, and many more items created from the sheep's wool. You could spend hours looking at the exhibits and then go on a tour of the working part of the farm. If you like being creative, craft classes are offered in the fall and winter.

Some of the machinery used by Custom Woolen Mills in the manufacture of products for knitting, quilting, and spinning could be considered old. The spinning mule was made in 1910 and the five carding machines date from 1867 to 1910. The comforter sewing machine was constructed in the mid 1900s.

The comforters made at Custom Mills are filled with 100% pure, virgin, Canadian wool. Because it is grown in a cold climate, it is fluffier than foreign wool. For those who live in the snow belt, soft, warm wool covers are great to snuggle under on frosty winter nights.

CROSSFIELD

When you enter the town of Crossfield, you are on the highest point of land between Calgary and Edmonton. A two storey high mural of a cowboy riding a bucking bronco is painted on the wall of the Crossfield AG Foods. Their rodeo, held during the first week in July, is called Pete Knight Days in honour of a world famous Alberta cowboy of the 1930s.

Chapter 3
Spruce Grove to Grande Cache

The section of Alberta opened up by this stretch of highway is excellent for fishermen, hunters, photographers, and hikers. Many of the lakes are stocked and the Athabasca, Pembina, Smoky, Wildhay, North Saskatchewan, and Macleod Rivers have fish ranging from grayling to giant pike. Deer, moose, elk, and bear roam the Edson area.

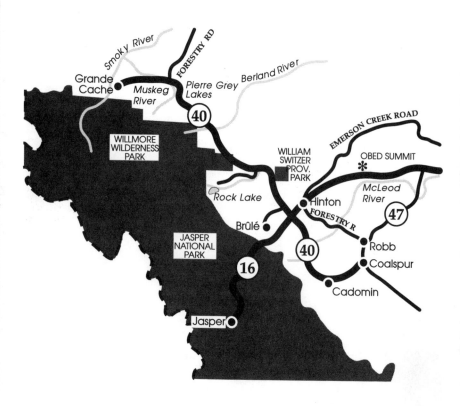

For a treasure hunt for some 60 million year old fossils, travel west on Highway #16 to Highway #770, then turn south. Follow the road to the Genessee corner, go west for three kilometres (1.8 miles) south 1.5 kilometres (one mile), and west again 1.5 kilometres to a small bridge. From here, a footpath leads to fossil beds along the North Saskatchewan River. Crack the flat, shale-like pieces of rock and you may expose an extinct plant. You can't keep the remains, but you can have fun exploring the area.

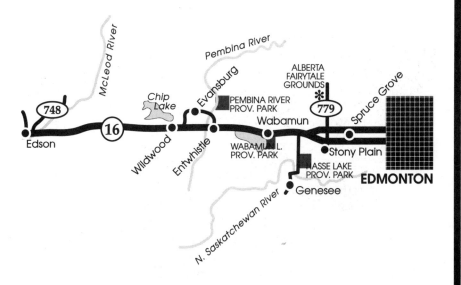

Spruce Grove to Seba Beach

SPRUCE GROVE

Spruce Grove is the site of the Kokusai Kaiyou Japanese High School, the first world-wide branch of the International High School of Marine Sciences, Ogasa, Japan. When the school's administrators decided to open a branch in another country, the president of the school spent months looking for an appropriate site in Australia, New Zealand, and other countries. She chose Spruce Grove after seeing commercials on television advertising the building of log homes in the area.

The school was opened in 1987, and 23 grade eleven students from Japan arrive for each four-month session. They learn life skills, English, and social studies and have the opportunity to partake in a different culture.

If you enjoy hiking, the Participark, which runs east/west through the centre of Spruce Grove, has 14 hectares (35 acres) of natural woodland to ramble through.

Ten kilometres (six miles) south of Spruce Grove on Golden Spike Road (turn south at Zender Ford) is the Parkland Exotic Pet Farm. There is a wide variety of birds and animals. Your children can ride a llama or miniature horse and the whole family can have their picture taken with any of the animals.

STONY PLAIN

The first homesteader arrived in the Dogrump Creek area in 1881 and happily took the name of the creek for the community. Eleven years later, one disgruntled citizen, who disliked the name Dogrump Creek, applied for it to be changed to Stony Plain.

Stony Plain's first sheriff was sworn in in 1907. Soon after he assumed duty, he chained the wheel of a railway locomotive to the tracks. It was his way of inducing the railroad to pay its taxes. The wheel, chain, and track are on a monument in front of the Multicultural Centre.

Stony Plain's Multicultural Centre is in the old high school, built in 1924, at 5411 51st Street. If you are hungry, or merely want to sample food from a past era, drop in to the Homesteader's Kitchen, where you can taste homemade pioneer and ethnic food. After

Locomotive wheel, chain, and track, Stony Plain

lunch, visit the craft store and settler's cabin, where you will see demonstrations of crafts and skills used by early immigrants.

Oppertshauser House is on the same grounds as the school. This residence was erected in 1910 by Henry Oppertshauser, a prominent businessman who had immigrated from Germany. Today, the dwelling is home to one of the few rural galleries in Alberta.

Shikaoi Park, Stony Plain

Stroll along the streets of Stony Plain and examine historic buildings. One, St. Matthew's Lutheran Church, is fashioned from fieldstone and has large, stained glass windows. It is the oldest Lutheran Church of the Missouri Synod in western Canada. (The Lutheran Church-Missouri Synod was founded in 1847 by German immigrants in the United States who wanted to keep their evangelical Lutheranism and who wanted to rule themselves.)

Visit the Japanese-inspired Shikaoi Park on the corner of 49th Street and 51st Avenue. The park was created to honour Stony Plain's sister city, Shikaoi, after representatives from the two communities signed a Sistership Relations Agreement in 1985. It has a little pond, a gazebo, trees, flowers, and benches to relax on.

That castle on the north side of Highway #16, opposite Stony Plain, is the site of the Andrew Wolf Wines Company. Have lunch in the picnic area and examine the giant casks which are positioned near the tables, beside the highway, and in the park-

Andrew Wolf Wines, Stony Plain

ing lot. Let your children play in the playground or visit the small animal zoo on the grounds. You are welcome to tour the business, sample some of the wine, and make purchases from their store.

Andrew Wolf

Andrew Wolf was born in Hungary and immigrated to Canada with his family at the age of five. He co-founded the family business in 1961, under the name Andrés Wine and originated the pop wine Baby Duck. In 1978, he established Andrew Wolf Wine Cellars, and he moved them to Stony Plain in 1984. He runs the business with his wife and two children. • The winery employs a traditional procedure for winemaking, and the liquid is aged in 100 year old French vats. They were the first to introduce "heat and drink" spiced wine and to open private wine stores in Alberta.

Take a drive to the Alberta Fairytale Grounds, whether you have children or not. Head north of Stony Plain on Highway #779 for 6.4 kilometres (four miles), turn west and continue for 3.2 kilometres (2 miles), then north for 1.6 kilometres (one mile) to the grounds. The park opened in 1988 and is located on 10 hectares (25 acres) of woodland. Asphalt trails guide you to the separate scenes.

Fairytale Mill, Alberta Fairytale Grounds

Expect a slight delay when you arrive. Each tale takes about 10 minutes to tell, so you may have to wait until the group ahead has had a chance to listen to the first story before you enter. The little buildings are well-built and colourful and have white picket fences around them. Benches are set in front so you can sit and enjoy each play. Press a button and the fairy tale will begin. Doors on the front of the house open and the story is played out for you by way of dolls and settings that rotate in front of the opening.

Everyone who visits the grounds will see a favourite from childhood. Some of the more popular plays are "Sleeping Beauty," "Hansel and Gretel," "Cinderella," and "Snow White."

Lake Eden is west of Stony Plain, with hills for the beginner and excellent runs for more advanced skiiers. Summertime sports include swimming, fishing, hiking, and camping.

For a treasure hunt for some 60 million year old fossils, return to Highway #16 and continue west to Highway #770, then turn south. Follow the road to the Genessee corner, go west for three kilometres (1.8 miles), south 1.5 kilometres (one mile), and west again 1.5 kilome-

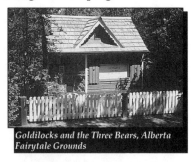

Goldilocks and the Three Bears, Alberta Fairytale Grounds

tres to a small bridge. From here, a footpath leads to fossil beds along the North Saskatchewan River. Crack the flat, shale-like pieces of rock and you may expose an extinct plant. You can't keep the remains, but you can have fun exploring the area.

LAKE WABAMUN

Further west on Highway #16 is Lake Wabamun. Three coal-fired power plants along the lake serve an area from Edmonton to Hinton. Because of the warm water piped into the lake from the plants, portions of the lake remain ice free in the winter. This has prompted many waterfowl and other birds to remain longer than usual in the fall. Wigeon, Canada geese, white-winged scoters, and common loons have been sighted in December. Other birds, like mallards, coots, and shovelers, have also become residents.

White-winged scoter

Along this shore, the mist scenes from *Blood Clan*, written and produced by Glynis Whiting and starring Gordon Pinsent, were filmed.

Sailboats, Seba Beach Regatta

The Village of Seba Beach is on the west shore of Lake Wabamun. The Edmonton Yacht Club operates out of a large club house in the village. In their yard are the area's first RCMP headquarters, built in the early 1890s. These historical cabins can be rented for the summer season. Be on the dock on the August long weekend to watch decorated sailboats pass by in the water parade during the Seba Beach Regatta.

Evansburg to Edson

EVANSBURG AND ENTWISTLE

Evansburg and Entwistle share the Pembina River Provincial Park, with its 140 campsites. Visitors enjoy swimming, hiking, picnicking, and fishing. A large variety of birds and animals make their homes in the tall stands of aspen and spruce.

The town of Evansburg was incorporated with the discovery of coal and the establishment of a mine by the Pembina Coal Company. The mine closed in 1936, but the community survived because of the growth of agriculture, forestry, oil, and gas industries.

Grouch

Evansburg has a Grouch of the Year award. Nominations are made, with the first round of voting deciding the top three candidates. A second vote chooses the winner. The new grouch has the responsibility of upholding the image of a grumpy coal miner, as a reminder of Evansburg's mining history. He, or she, is presented with a licence to criticize, complain, harass, grumble, and antagonize. The "winner" also receives a trophy, a grouch pin, a village pin, and a sign for his lawn.

Wildwood is Canada's Bingo Capital of incorporated communities with populations of less than 500. Seven different charities book the town hall for more than 140 bingos a year.

In most years, Wildwood also holds the title of being the smallest community in Canada to have its own trade coin. The Wildwood Elks Lodge issues a coin which is recognized by numismatists around the world. Each new coin depicts an aspect of the district and celebrates World Coin Week. You can purchase the coins at the tourist information booth, and most of the businesses in town accept them as legal tender.

Chip Lake, just west of Wildwood, boasts a 61 acre park with a boat launch, cleaning table, and playground. The lands around the lake are an unofficial wildlife sanctuary for Canada geese, snow geese, ducks, pelicans, swans, and other birds that inhabit or use them as a stop-over point on their migrations.

Chip Lake was shortened from Buffalo Chip Lake and at times in its history it was also burdened with the names Bull Dung Lake and Dirt Lake. While there, watch for moose, deer, and elk. Also be on the lookout for Dippy, the Chip Lake Monster. He has been described as having a long neck, small head, and large body and has been "observed" gliding through the waters along the banks of the recreation area.

The History of Dippy

According to legend, Dippy is an offspring of Nessie, the Loch Ness Monster. Many years ago, fear that the loch could not support more than one monster drove scientists to remove two eggs from the waters. Lake Okanagan in British Columbia was chosen as a new site and they were transported by steamer across the Atlantic Ocean and then put on two separate trains bound for Lake Okanagan (to make sure at least one made it.) • The first train arrived without trouble, but the engine of the second, with the egg inside, derailed at Chip Lake and was never recovered. The egg at Lake Okanagan hatched and Ogopogo has since become almost as famous as its mother. The egg in Chip Lake was forgotten until May of 1986, when a creature, resembling Nessie, was seen in the waters. Many speculate that Dippy hatched from that lost egg.

Lodgepole pine received their name from the Natives who used the tall, straight timbers as poles for their teepees or lodges. These trees grow well in the area, and shelter the gold-thread plant, which is rare in Alberta.

EDSON

The old school, constructed in 1913, now houses Edson's Red Brick Arts Centre. It was saved from demolition by the Edson Cultural Heritage Organization (ECHO), and a school museum, art gallery, theatre, dance studio, and gift shop are now the tenants in the renovated structure.

Other artifacts from Edson's history have been assembled in the Galloway Museum. This museum is in the railway station at Centennial Park. Also in the park are a mounted military jet, a restored caboose, the tourist information booth, and a picnic area.

If you plan to stay a few days in the area, stop at the tourist booth and pick up your "Travelcard." You will also receive a pamphlet with the names of businesses in town which will give you a discount when you use your card.

As you drive between Edson and Hinton, look for the Obed Summit sign. When you see it, you will be at the highest point on the Yellowhead Highway between Winnipeg, Manitoba, and the Pacific Ocean. The elevation is 1163.9 metres (3818.6 feet) above sea level. Everything goes downhill from here.

The Obed Mountain Coal Company, at the summit, is an open-pit mine which offers tours of its operation. However, you have to book them in Hinton. After Obed, you will be travelling with the mountains in front of you.

Emerson Lakes Road

An alternate route from Edson to Hinton is the Emerson Lakes road. Take Highway #748 north of Edson for 32 kilometres (19 miles). Watch closely for the Emerson Lake sign because the turn west is almost a hairpin. This road was built and is maintained by Weldwood of Canada. Since it is used for log hauling, beware of logging trucks and turn on your lights. • Along the drive are numbered yellow signs. The numerals begin at Hinton, so they decrease the further you go. Watch for cougars in this area. • West central Alberta has its own version of hoodoos. Near yellow sign 61, about 30 kilometres (18 miles) from the turn, is the Wild Sculpture Trail. You can hike to the sandstone towers carved by the wind and water and past three beautiful glacial lakes: Beaver Lake, Little Sundance Lake, and Sundance Lake. Each has a campsite. Maybe you will sight a beaver swimming in the waters or working on its house. • As you approach yellow sign 51, you will be able to see the bluish green of one of the six Emerson Lakes through the trees. Pause at the small campsite and enjoy the serenity of the valley. Gasoline-powered boats are not allowed on the lakes, so your tranquil interlude will not be disturbed. • Canyon Creek hiking trail is between yellow signs 18 and 19. Walk the 1.5 kilometre (0.9 mile) trail along the edge of the canyon and watch the ground drop 91 metres (296 feet) into a valley in the distance. • When you arrive at the end of the road, turn south towards Hinton. Before reaching the town, you will cross the Athabasca River on a one lane bridge (yield to oncoming traffic).

Hinton and District

Hinton emerged in the early 1900s when fur and timber lured the first settlers to this area. The Grand Trunk Railway came in 1912, and Hinton grew. Coal mines opened and Alberta's first pulp and paper mill was built in 1955. Recognized as a town in 1958, Hinton has a population of over 5,000.

Forestry Museum, Hinton

The Forest Technology School, on Switzer Drive, is the first to educate students about the earth's renewable resources. The Forestry Museum, situated on the grounds of the Forest Technology School, was organized to preserve Alberta's forest management history. If you wish to tour the school or museum, contact the school's main office.

Green Square is home to one of the largest chessboards in the world. The board is 9.8 by 9.8 metres (32 by 32 feet) wide. The chess pieces are animated and dressed in 18th century costumes. They walk to their appropriate squares. The Knights gallop up on horseback, dismount, and stride to their positions. Two carriages appear and out step the Kings in their period clothing. They assist the Queens from the coaches and escort them to their reigning squares. Then the game is about to begin.

This live chess theatre is held outside during Hinton's Multicultural Festival in September. The moves are from a famous chess game from history. A narrator describes the game as players step among the chess "pieces" and move them to different squares. Only three or four such live chess games are held throughout the world.

CADOMIN

Travel south of Hinton on Highway #40 to reach Cadomin. There is good elk hunting in the area. The pavement is narrow, but traffic is minimal and the mountain scenery spectacular. Watch for the two small waterfalls on the west side.

A few kilometres south of the falls is Cardinal River Coals at Luscar. Stop and view the large open-pit mining operation from the roadside turnout. The excavation has exposed varying layers of soil beneath ground level.

Luscar

The first Luscar Collieries mine was opened here in 1921, and the town of Luscar soon appeared. When the mine closed in 1956, Luscar quickly became a ghost town. The houses were either moved to Edson or torn down. The mine was reopened in 1969 by Cardinal River Coals, but no town was built.

Cadomin is a quiet, peaceful mountain town. The Mountain Road General Store and Hole-in-the-Wall Cafe are in one large building with a lone gas pump out front.

The Coal Branch

When coal was in great demand to power steam locomotives, coal towns and mines were plentiful in the Coal Branch area. Cadomin, with 2,500 people, was the largest of these towns. The introduction of diesel powered engines in 1952 signalled the demise of the industry. Luscar, Leyland, Mountain Park, Coalspur, and Mercoal soon disappeared. Cadomin was officially declared a ghost town but was saved from total closure when a rock quarry was opened to supply an Edmonton based cement plant with limestone. • The coal mining era has left a legacy, though — a fire that never dies. In 1919, an underground fire broke out in one of the mines near Coalspur and it could not be extinguished. The shaft had to be shut down and a new one opened. The fire is still smoldering today.

The store has the potential to be a museum. Shelves are brimming with antiques, including different types of irons that had to be heated on the wood stove before use. Old photos, scythes, sickles, miners' lanterns, saws, and faded advertising posters hang on the walls. Wander through the aisles or rest on the park bench beside the book display.

For the rock hound, fossils have been found in the limestone quarry at Cadomin. A few kilometres southwest of Cadomin, at the McLeod River, hundreds of years of flowing waters have cut through the sandstones and shales of the Nikanassin Range. Three hundred million year old Mississippian sedimentary rock has been uncovered.

Six kilometres (3.7 miles) south of Cadomin, on the Cardinal River Road, is the Whitehorse Creek Campground. If you like hiking or overnight camping, and would enjoy a nice relaxing soak in a hot springs afterwards, try the 41 kilometre (24 mile) trail from the campground, through the Fiddle Pass, and on to Miette Hot Springs in Jasper National Park. You will see superb mountain scenery, valleys, meadows, streams, and Whitehorse Falls (a 3.2 kilometre (two mile) side trip).

Continue from the Whitehorse Creek campground to the Cadomin Caves. While the cavities are fascinating for spelunking, they are also dangerous. Anyone exploring the caves should be well-prepared and must carry the proper equipment. Good physical condition is another must since it is a long, arduous struggle to the entrance. For a guided tour of the caves, phone (403) 852-4012.

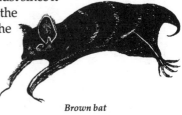

The most famous of the caves, Cadomin Cave, is the only known site in Alberta where brown bats hibernate.

Brown bat

Past the caves is the town of Mountain Park. It was abandoned in the 1950s and very little is left to mark its existence. If you aren't into ghost towns, go there for the view. Mountain Park is higher than the tree line, at 1,908 metres (6,200 feet) above sea level. The terrain is great for dirt bikes and ATVs.

COALSPUR AND ROBB

Back at Cadomin, continue on Highway #40 to the junction of #47. Turn onto the gravelled #47 towards Robb. You will pass the Coalspur campsite and return to pavement. As you take the curve to the east, look straight ahead and up the hill. You will see a coal chute, left over from the days of surface mining.

If you want to take a closer look at the relic, continue along the highway to the junction with a roadway that leads to the base of the hill. Park there and walk across the railway tracks, past the large pile of coal and the remains of coal cars, and up the hill. It is a steep climb to the chute. Watch the ground; about half way up, you'll find yourself walking on coal.

Coal Chute, Coalspur

At the top, another car, in reasonably good condition, sits by itself. Don't trip on the old tracks hidden in the grass. These lead from the side of the hill, where the miners extracted the coal, to the chute. Chunks of coal lie on the ground and you can see seams of black in the hillside. There is a vast difference between mining operations of the past and the new mining facilities at Luscar.

At Robb you can cut across country to Hinton on the Forestry Trunk Road or take Highway #47 to Highway #16 at Edson.

Brule to Grande Cache

BRULE

Be sure to gas up in Hinton as there are no services for the next 141 kilometres (87 miles). From Hinton go 6.5 kilometres (four miles) north on Highway #40 to the turn to Brule. At one time, Brule was a large mining town. Like most communities in the area, however, it became a ghost town when the mines closed. Many of the houses were moved to Edmonton. It has slowly made a comeback and now has some large new homes.

Take your ATVs to the Brule Lake sand dunes. Old telegraph poles and the remains of the Grand Trunk Pacific station have been buried by the constantly changing dunes. Maybe you will find a sign of them.

ATHABASCA TOWER AND WILLIAM SWITZER PROVINCIAL PARK

Continue on Highway #40 for about 14 kilometres (8.5 miles) to the turn to the Nordic Centre and the Athabasca Tower. The long, steep, narrow road climbs continuously, passing the upper parking lot and lodge for the Nordic Centre at about kilometre three (mile 1.8). The centre has cross country skiing, biatholon and telemark facilities, night skiing, and a 1,000 metre (3,250 foot) luge track.

If you aren't afraid of heights, obtain permission from a forest ranger and climb the steps to the top of the tower at the summit. The view is breathtaking. Hang gliding is a popular sport in the area and you might be treated to the sight of one floating through the air below.

William Switzer Provincial Park is at kilometre 19 (mile 11.8) on Highway #40. Tales have been told of monster pike in the depths of Jarvis Lake. Hike the many trails and study the plants and wildlife with naturalists. To learn about nature and how to survive in the wilderness, contact the Blue Lake Centre at the park to book a weekend, or longer, course.

ROCK LAKE AND WILLMORE WILDERNESS PARK

Back on Highway #40, watch for the turn to Rock Lake and the staging area for Willmore Wilderness Park, about 10 kilometres (six miles) from the park exit. They are about 32 kilometres (20 miles) west on the gravel road.

At the Rock Lake campground, the mountains reflect in the brilliant blue of the lake and hiking trails follow the shores. For fishermen, the lake is alive with brook trout and Rocky Mountain whitefish while the Wildhay River teems with dolly varden. Hikers will enjoy the five kilometres (three miles) of trails around the lake. The only drawback to the campground is that the water has to be boiled for ten minutes before using. Bring your own supply of drinking water if you plan to stay a few days.

The staging area for Willmore Wilderness Park is just west of the lake and you can walk or drive to it. Many outfitters operate out of Hinton and Grande Cache, so you can book ahead for an excursion into the park on horseback. Or you can bring your

Creek at Rock Lake

own horses with you. Hikers should use a map and inform someone of their plans before venturing into the wilderness.

Thirty-five kilometres (21.5 miles) past the Rock Lake turn, you enter the Woodland Caribou winter range. If you are driving this road between November and May, watch for animals crossing the road or in the area for the next 32 kilometres (20 miles).

Two kilometres north, you cross the Berland River. There is a recreation area on the west side if you wish to stop. One of the few haunts of the wolverine in Alberta is along the Berland River. The Smoky River, just north of the Berland, is one of the best rivers in the province for landing arctic grayling.

Do you like to pick huckleberries and blueberries? Twelve kilometres (7.5 miles) north of the Berland River is a northeast running road, through the Huckleberry Tower Road Wildlife Sanctuary, to the Huckleberry Tower. Follow it for about 34 kilometres (21 miles) and you will be in berry country. Note: the tower sign is not on the highway; it is on the gravel road.

GRANDE CACHE

Grande Cache is 1,292 metres (4,200 feet) above sea level at the base of Grande Mountain. Early trappers stored or cached their furs here during the winter, hence the name.

Charter a jet boat or take a guided raft tour on the Smoky River. The Smoky and Sulphur Rivers offer a challenge for experienced kayakers and canoeists. One leg of the World Championship Riverboat Racing series is run on the Smoky, between Grande Cache and Peace River.

Grande Cache Lake, Pierre Grey's Lakes, and Victor Lake are a trout fisherman's paradise. For fly-fishing, try Sheep Creek, Muskeg River, or the Big Berland.

Artists, photographers, and golfers will appreciate the 9-hole golf course, with its background of mountains and clear blue skies. For hang gliding enthusiasts, both the Grande and Hamel Mountains are accessible by road. If you are a serious hang glider, enter the annual Grande Cache Hang Gliding Championships, held in June.

Hell's Gate, Grande Cache

To get to Hell's Gate, follow Highway #40 north of town, cross the blue bridge over the Smoky River, and turn left. Seven kilometres (four miles) down the gravel road you will come to a campground. Don't be surprised to see a number of horses, as this is another staging area for Willmore Wilderness Park.

Walk towards the Willmore Wilderness Park sign then follow the path to the left. You are warned that there are steep cliffs and you walk at your own risk. Follow the path and you will see where the different colours of the Sulphur and Smoky rivers join and where they have cut a deep canyon in the rocks.

The path is narrow and sometimes you are beside the edge, sometimes you are in bush. You can walk onto parts of rock that jut out over the waters to take pictures, but be careful when the wind blows.

A wide variety of animals roam the forests around Grande Cache. Caribou, lynx, elk, moose, wolves, grizzly bears, mountain sheep, and mountain goats are just a few.

In the summer you can pick wild strawberries south of the town, at the Sulphur River Canyon. In the winter, Grande Mountain provides good telemark terrain, and heli-skiing and cat-skiing facilities are available. Pierre Grey Lakes has three excellent cross-country ski trails. There are many trails in the Grande Cache region for snowmobilers. For photographers, the Huckleberry Tower area plays host to large caribou herd migrations each year.

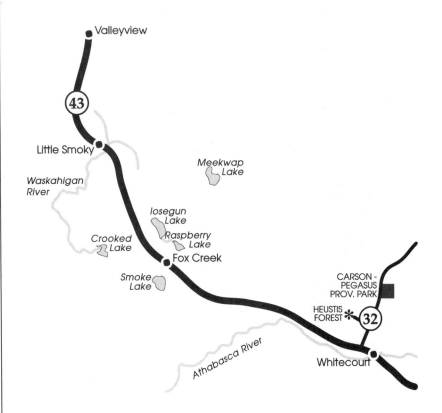

Chapter 4
Swan Hills to St. Albert to Valleyview

This section of Alberta has a wide variety of unusual plant, insect, and animal life. Some species are hundreds of kilometres from their natural environment. Again, as in most parts of Alberta, there is an abundance of good fishing and hunting.

To view an interesting wooded area, go northwest of Whitecourt to Highway #32 and turn north. A five kilometre (three mile) drive brings you to the E.S. Huestis Demonstration Forest.

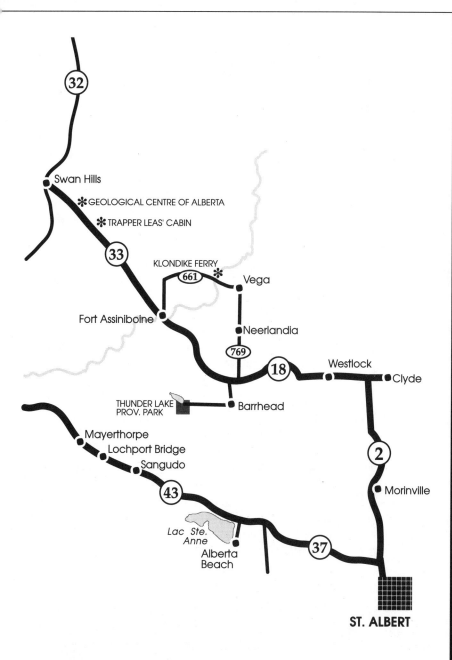

There are a number of private and provincial campgrounds in the Valleyview area. Four of them are located on Sturgeon Lake west of the town, where you can fish for lake whitefish, walleye, northern pike, and perch.

Swan Hills to Barrhead

The highest elevation in the Swan Hills is 1,128 metres (3,666 feet). They are wetter and cooler than most of Alberta's foothills. Many old seismic and logging roads crisscross the hills, making these hills relatively easy for naturalists and archaeologists to explore.

Twenty-five kilometres (15 miles) west of the town of Swan Hills is the Goose Mountain Ecological Reserve. Goose Mountain has a unique blend of rain forest, cordilleran (mountain), and subarctic plants. Just as dominant on the west side of the mountain as in the British Columbia coastal rain forest is the three-leaved false mitrewort. White rhododendron, red elderberry, alpine speedwell, and yellow anemone fall into the cordilleran category, while some subarctic plants are trailing raspberry and leather-leaf. A number of ferns are also present.

For those into entomology, an unusual insect population inhabits the mountain. *Ebria metallica*, a ground beetle of the B.C. coastal mountains, is present, as are several leaf mining flies.

In 1918, a bed of fossil fresh-water mollusks was discovered on Wallace Mountain. Numerous other fossils have been found, including crocodile teeth, twigs from *Metasequoia*, a class of needleleaf tree, and many bone fragments.

The Alberta Special Waste Treatment Plant, North America's first such facility, is seven kilometres (4.3 miles) north of the town of Swan Hills and 10 kilometres (six miles) east of the highway. It was designed to treat and dispose of most types of special waste created in Alberta. The plant is rapidly becoming a tourist attraction, with many people from Canada and the U.S. visiting it each year.

Special Waste Treatment Plant

The Alberta Special Waste Treatment Plant was officially opened on September 11, 1987 and is the first of its kind in North America. It can treat approximately 23,000 metric tons (25,555 tons) of waste annually. • Special or hazardous wastes are those that cannot be disposed of through burning, a sewage system, or in landfills. They fall into four categories: corrosive, which can dissolve metals or burn skin; reactive, which react when combined with water or other materials; ignitable, which catch fire easily; and environmental contaminants such as lead, mercury and pesticides. • The waste is analyzed, then put through seven treatment processes which break down the complex molecular structures of the chemicals into non-toxic compounds. Those that can be are incinerated, while others are securely stored. • The plant does not treat radioactive or infectious waste or explosives.

If you love snowmobiling, try the Krause Lake Snowmobile Area. Special trails run through the town and spread out into the hills. They are regulated by the Alberta Forest Service and are open to anyone.

The hills are popular for moose, deer, and bear hunting. However, the Swan Hills grizzly is a protected animal.

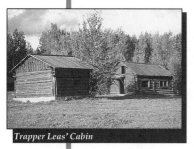
Trapper Leas' Cabin

Trapper Leas' Cabin is about 30 kilometres (18 miles) southeast of Swan Hills on Highway #33. Leas set up a trapline and built the smaller of the two buildings in 1938. He constructed the second one in 1943. Also in that year, he trapped the greatest number of wolves in the province and was named "Wolf King of Alberta." There is a small campsite beside the two cabins and a snowmobile loading ramp for those who wish to have some winter fun.

Five kilometres (three miles) south of Trapper Leas' is a sign on the left side of the road indicating the three kilometre (1.8 mile) trail to the centre of Alberta. To reach the heart of the province, just follow the brown and yellow "Centre" signs, or arrows, through the bush. At the end of the trail is a white picket fence around a bright orange survey marker. It is quiet and peaceful in the centre of the bush and there are picnic tables for those who wish to bring a lunch. To return to the highway, follow the yellow and brown "G. T." signs.

FORT ASSINIBOINE

In 1824, Alberta's first man-made pack trail was cut from Edmonton to Fort Assiniboine, which had been established in 1823. The road was 113 kilometres (70 miles) long and ran through where Barrhead, Lac La Nonne, Riviere Qui Barre, and St. Albert are today. At Fort Assiniboine, a large replica of the original post has been constructed.

Instead of driving south to Barrhead on the highway, take a little extra time and head north of Fort Assiniboine for about 20 kilometres (12 miles), turn east on #661 and cross the Athabasca River on the Klondike Ferry. The ferry

Fort Assiniboine

was originally set up at Fort Assiniboine, but was eventually moved to its present site and given a new name — Vega Ferry. It operates seven days a week, from break-up of the river in the spring to freeze-up in the fall.

Klondike Trail

The only all-Canadian route to the Klondike, sometimes called the "back door route," or the "Overland route," began in Alberta. When news of the Klondike Gold Rush reached the outside world, many prospective miners studied their maps and saw that Edmonton was the town closest to the gold fields that could be reached by rail. They arrived at the outpost and requested guides and supplies for their journey, not bothered by the fact that the Klondike lay 2,400 kilometres (1,500 miles) away, across unexplored land. • Seventeen hundred prospectors headed north. Many went to Athabasca Landing and some followed the water route up to the Mackenzie River, across the Richardson Mountains to Dawson City. 565 of these successfully completed the trip. Others headed northwest from Athabasca Landing, ending up at Lesser Slave Lake. •But the majority headed across country on the Chalmer's or Klondike Trail. It had been partially cleared by a group of government men, with T.W. Chalmers as the engineer. The Klondikers travelled through Lac La Nonne, across the Athabasca River, and on to Fort Assiniboine. From there they headed north to the west end of Lesser Slave Lake and then to Peace River Crossing, Dunvegan, and Fort St. John. After that, it was a matter of slashing their way across two passes and following more than six rivers until, at last, they arrived at the Yukon River and were able to float down it to the Klondike. Not everyone pursued this exact route and not everyone succeeded in reaching their chosen destination. • Some records indicate that less than 200 prospectors made it to the Klondike over the Klondike Trail. Many detoured to the gold field at Omineca, 35 died along the way, and the remainder returned to Edmonton.

NEERLANDIA, THUNDER LAKE PROVINCIAL PARK, AND BARRHEAD

Continue east to Vega, then south to Neerlandia. In 1912, Dutch settlers began the small, exclusively Dutch community and named it after their home country. To see an example of splendid country architecture, drive by the Neerlandia Church.

As you drive south through Barrhead on Highway #33 watch for the giant blue heron statue on the west side, just past the junction with Highway #18. For years, blue herons have nested on an island on Thunder Lake and the town has adopted them as their symbol.

If you are a naturalist or just enjoy nature, head to Thunder Lake Provincial Park, 21 kilometres (12.5 miles) west of Barrhead. A large variety of plants prosper in the park, including golden saxifrage, purple pea vine, water arum, touch-me-not, snake-root, agrimony, enchanters nightshade, and Indian pipe.

Westlock to St. Albert

Dick Adkins does not advertise his museum, so the only way you will notice it, as you approach Westlock, is to watch the south side of the road for two rows of wooden animals lining a driveway. This driveway is the entrance to Dick Adkins' yard — and his museum.

All the animals and accessories were designed, cut, and painted by Mr. Adkins. Some are from fairy tales, some are from history, and others are nature's own. There is Babe the blue ox, an old cart called the Red River Special, and a horse pulling a travois. Cows, buffalo, elephants, moose, deer, goats, and wolves stand side by side. In his garage is a wooden Santa Claus in a sleigh. At Christmas, he hooks up the sleigh to one of the deer and poses them by the highway.

When you have examined the animals and your children have ridden the rocking elephant, Mr. Adkins will guide you to his back yard. Old plows, wagons, and log cabins are positioned in the trees. Some of the equipment was bought by his father and Dick can recite the years they were purchased and how long they were used.

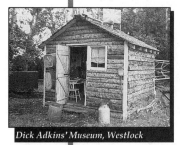

Dick Adkins' Museum, Westlock

Walk into the homesteader's cabin, with its wood stove and rocking chair, or visit the blacksmith's shop and see the many tools needed in a smithy. In another building, Dick stores his milk bottle collection and the antique machinery used to fill the bottles. He will demonstrate the filling process for you while he proudly displays what he claims to be the largest milk bottle collection in the world. Then he will show you his treasure trove of newspapers, one of which is an *Edmonton Bulletin* dated 1885.

Since retiring from farming, Mr. Adkins has spent many years working on his museum and he truly enjoys showing it to visitors. You are invited to eat your lunch in the picnic area in his yard and stay as long as you wish.

There are a number of private museums in the Westlock area with agriculture and pioneer displays. Check at the tourist booth for more information on them.

The Clyde Auctioneers hold an auction every Wednesday night, from the end of August to the end of June. An antique auction is held on the last Saturday of each month and there are special public sales throughout the year. One of these special auctions is the annual gun and hunting equipment sale at the end of August.

The tall spire you see gleaming in the sunlight belongs to the St. Jean Baptiste Roman Catholic Church of Morinville. Completed in 1893, the church and the adjacent rectory were declared historical sites in 1974.

St. Jean Baptiste Roman Catholic Church, Morinville

On 101st Avenue, you will find the Morinville Historic and Cultural Centre. Originally constructed as a convent in 1909, it was designated as an historical site in 1978. It now houses the town's museum and is used by many community services.

St. Albert Trail

One of the oldest trails in Alberta is the St. Albert Trail. It began as a a route followed by Natives, then the early settlers heading north developed it into a road for their supply wagons. The 66 kilometre (40 mile) trail begins at St. Albert and ends at Clyde, although the paved highway from Edmonton to St. Albert is also called the St. Albert Trail.

ST. ALBERT

The city of St. Albert is an historic site. It was founded by Father Albert Lacombe, "the Black-Robed Voyageur," in 1861, as a mission for the Métis in the area. The mission was named after Father Lacombe's patron saint.

Monument to Father Lacombe, St. Albert

Though Father Lacombe spent only five years at St. Albert, he contributed greatly to the advancement of the mission and the Métis. His first duty was to erect a log chapel overlooking the Sturgeon River. Once it was completed, he oversaw the building of Alberta's first saw mill, its first bridge, and its first horse-drawn grist mill — all while administering to the spiritual needs of his congregation.

Father Lacombe's log chapel was moved from its original site in 1871 and was used as a sacristy and storage shed. Some restoration was done in 1927, with about 40 per cent of the original material being replaced. A protective brick shell was constructed around it and it was used as a museum for the next fifty years. After being designated a Provincial Historic Resource in 1977, the shell was removed and the chapel was returned to the hill above the Sturgeon River.

Grandin House, St. Albert

Next door, in contrast to the tiny chapel, is Grandin House. It's a massive, three storey structure which was completed in 1887. Initially, it was to be operated as a Grey Nun's hospital, but the design was unsuitable. It became the official residence of the Bishop Vital J. Grandin. On the other side of the chapel is the St. Albert Parish Church, constructed in 1922. Walk behind the church and view the crypt where the body of Father Lacombe lies in honour. Then take the long, flower-lined path to the grotto, a replica of la Grotto des Apparitions de Lourdes (the Lourdes Grotto) in France.

In 1862, Father Lacombe erected a bridge where the Perron Street bridge is today. Just north is the Founder's Promenade, a red rock sidewalk that winds up the hill in Mission Park. Along the walkway, in the grass, are plaques with the names of the city's founders and the years they arrived.

The city hall provides a contrast to all the historic buildings in St. Albert. St. Albert Place is on the banks of the Sturgeon River. Designed by Douglas Cardinal, this show piece of modern architecture is a brown brick structure with three levels and many contours. Inside is a museum, the Arden theatre, arts and crafts displays, and a library.

Alberta Beach to Mayerthorpe

Alberta Beach

To reach Alberta Beach from St. Albert, go north on Highway #2, turn west on Highway #37 and follow it to Gunn, then turn south. Alberta Beach, on Lac Ste. Anne, was incorporated in 1920 and is one of the oldest and largest summer villages in Alberta.

During the summer, the Alberta Beach Summer Playhouse stages dinner theatre productions. They are held Thursday, Friday, and Saturday evenings with a Saturday matinee at GJ's Recreation Ranch. Phone (403) 924-3309 to make the required advance reservations and to get directions to the ranch.

The Pioneer Museum and Archives is in an historic church on the main street, but the one you really must see is The Alberta Beach Museum, crowded into a private yard east of town. When the paved road turns west into Alberta Beach, take the gravel road heading east and follow it about 1.5 kilometres (0.9 miles) to the museum.

You will not see another exhibit like this in Alberta or probably in Canada. The owners have been labouring at their venture since the 1960s. You will be taken on a slow, informative circuit that gives you the opportunity to examine the museum in its entirety.

A two metre (six foot) tall heart, created from cement and decorated with colourful shells, stands near the house. "Be My Valentine" is written across it and it is pierced by an arrow. Well trodden paths lead under archways and past rocks from the Frank Slide, old grave markers, buildings filled with oddments, and cabinets crammed with shells and starfish. Nestled in the trees in one corner is a Native village with a teepee and many artifacts. In another corner, you will find a cement and rock church.

There is no charge for the tour, but donations are appreciated.

If you are at Lac Ste. Anne on the long weekend in August, attend Alberta Beach's annual Polynesian Days. The Alberta Beach Sailing Club presents a colourful sailing regatta and there is a hula competition, canoe races, the crowning of a Polynesian Queen, and a garden tractor and trike rodeo.

The largest annual pilgrimage in Canada is held at the Lac Ste. Anne Mission, in July. Over 15,000 worshippers from across Canada and the United States make the sacred expedition to participate in the six full days of religious celebration.

Devil's Lake

At one time, Lac Ste. Anne was thought to be cursed by evil spirits, and was fearfully called Devil's Lake. In 1843, Father Thibault, O.M.I. (Order of Mary Immaculate), blessed the lake, renamed it Ste. Anne, and established the first Roman Catholic Mission in Alberta. • Father Albert Lacombe spent nine years at the mission before beginning his travels through western Canada. In 1859, three Grey Nuns arrived in Edmonton from Montreal, and hastened to Lac St. Anne to assist Father Lacombe. They were the first educated European women to come to Alberta. • In July of 1889, 46 years after the blessing, Father Lestanc initiated the first Lac Ste. Anne Pilgrimage, with 200 people attending. The people listened to sermons, heard music, and walked into the blessed waters, in the belief that these things possessed curing powers.

When the name Deep Creek was rejected by the government, early settlers in the area rose to the occasion by selecting a name for their community in a unique manner. Three chose the first letter of each of their names: Sutton or Sides, Albers, and Gaskell; another took the first letter from her home town: Nanton; one letter came from the creek: Deep; and one was from the school district: Orangeville. They selected the U because they were "united" in the name.

The letters, when arranged together, spell the name Sangudo. The town overlooks the Pembina River Valley. If the fish aren't biting, try panning for gold in the river.

Rochfort Bridge

Ten kilometres (six miles) north of Sangudo is the Rochfort Bridge. At the time of its construction, it was the longest wooden bridge in North America. You can stand on the highway beside the towering north end and not see the south end.

At the town of Rochfort Bridge is the Rochfort Bridge Trading Post, in a log building on the north side of the highway. Inside is a small cafe and a huge selection of crafts: moccasins, suede handbags, ceramics, Native dolls, Inuit sculptures, birdhouses, sweaters, paintings, jewellery and much more.

Across from the turn into Rochfort Bridge is a gravel road heading south to the Paddle River Dam. There is a picnic area, a boat launch, good fishing, and a viewpoint at the reservoir.

Mayerthorpe is a town for horse lovers. Each year, a number of equestrian events are held. The annual Open Cutting Horse Competition is in May, as is the Wild and Wooly Horse Show and Rodeo. The challenging Open Hunter Jump Competition is staged in July.

Whitecourt to Valleyview

WHITECOURT

Northwest of Mayerthorpe on Highway #43 is Whitecourt, "Snowmobile Capital of Alberta." The Alberta Forest Service has developed three regional snowmobile trail systems in the woodland around Whitecourt. The markers along the trails are much like road signs.

E.S. Huestis Demonstration Forest

To view an interesting wooded area, go northwest of Whitecourt to Highway #32 and turn north. A five kilometre (three mile) drive brings you to the E.S. Huestis Demonstration Forest.

This working woodland covers 10 square kilometres (3.8 square miles) and you can drive the seven kilometres (4.3 miles) of roads to 17 interpretive sites within the area. Some of the sites display different forest management schemes, from commercial clear cutting and natural regeneration, to old, degenerating sections of forest. Each site has a write-up about the forest around it. You will see an old growth coniferous forest, a deciduous forest, spruce understory, spruce cutblock, topography and geology, and a beaver dam.

Forest management has been modelled after the idea that the harvesting of trees should match the new growth of trees. The Huestis forest was developed to help the public learn more about forest management.

FOX CREEK

Within the vicinity of Fox Creek are a number of excellent fishing lakes. Some can be reached by road, but others are for the more dedicated fisherman who is willing to drive an ATV or even walk to catch his limit.

Smoke Lake and Crooked Lake are west of Fox Creek. Smoke Lake has a campground, a boat launch, and fish cleaning tables. You can drive its perimeter if you wish to see some of the landscape. The lake has pike to 6.8 kilograms (15 pounds), jumbo whitefish to 5.5 kilograms (12 pounds) and walleye to 3.6 kilograms (eight pounds).

Crooked Lake is a considerable distance back in the bush. You leave your vehicle at Little Crooked Lake and from there, hike or ATV the last stretch. Do not attempt the drive in wet weather.

Isogun, Raspberry, Jerry, and Meekwap Lakes are northeast of Fox Creek. Isogun is the most popular of the lakes and it has the greatest variety of fish: perch, northern pike, walleye, lake whitefish, and tullibee. For non-anglers, there is also a campground, a boat launch, a picnic area, and a beach.

Jerry Lake has northern pike, while Raspberry Lake has northern pike and perch. You will have a 10-minute walk to get to Jerry Lake, but Raspberry is about 2.5 kilometres (1.5 miles) from the road. Meekwap is also a remote lake accessible by walking trails.

If you doubt that the drive and hike into these lakes is worth your time and energy, stop in at the Motor Vehicle License Office, situated in the Home Hardware Store, and see an 11.8 kilogram (26 pound) northern pike caught at Isogun.

Forest Blending

The area between Fox Creek and Valleyview is typical of a region where mountain and the northern boreal forests blend. White spruce and balsam fir are interspersed with muskeg, full of tamarack, black spruce and peat moss, usually found in the north. Lodgepole pine is indicative of the spruce forests of the mountains. • Also thriving here are plants native to this type of mixed forest, including 12 species of orchids. False mitreworts and devil's club, usually found in British Columbia, can be seen here. Pine-sap has been found in less than a dozen places in Alberta and twice in this area. • Big game hunting is very popular in this forest.

LITTLE SMOKY AND VALLEYVIEW

Little Smoky has a service station, a store, and a motel with cabins for rent. There are many old trails leading to isolated regions around the hamlet. You can bird watch, take pictures, be a rock hound, or just have a picnic. Watch for lynx, red fox, cougars, and even wolves while on your visit. If you are an amateur palaeontologist, you will know that few fossils have been found in the periphery of Little Smoky, but did you know that a mammoth tusk was once discovered along the Waskahigan River?

Four Seasons Flower and Garden Centre, Valleyview

When the pioneers moved into the area around 1916, they settled in what the natives called Mighkopower Seepesis, or Red Willow Creek. The town's name was changed from Red Willow to Valleyview in 1929, indicating the view of the valley left by the Sturgeon Creek.

Just before the town of Valleyview, there is a rest area with picnic tables, a tourist information booth, and a large parking lot.

Visit the Four Seasons Flower and Garden Centre on the main street, between 49th and 50th Avenues. In a fenced yard beside the shop is a miniature garden with flowers, paths, benches, an arched bridge, and a small church. The best time to visit is after the beginning of July.

There are a number of private and provincial campgrounds in the Valleyview area. Four of them are located on Sturgeon Lake west of the town, where you can fish for lake whitefish, walleye, northern pike, and perch.

Chapter 5
Slave Lake to Peace River

In an effort to add variety to Alberta's forests, unusual and exotic trees have been introduced into the province. Some are of commercial value, others are ornamental. One, the bur oak, has managed to survive as far north as Slave Lake and Peace River.

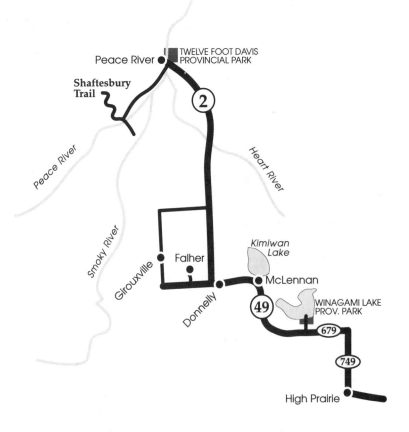

The bur oak, also known as the mossy-cup oak, earned its name from its acorns, which are encased in a fringed cup. This type of oak is hardy, with a rough crown, grooved bark, and wide, spreading branches. Deep notches, or sinuses, score the large leaves. The tree is popular for shade in parks and for its lumber. Watch for this new Albertan broadleaf as you travel this part of the province.

The Oak

Oaks do not grow well in areas of extreme cold. They grow slowly and live to be 200 to 300 years old. Generally, they are about 20 years old before they bear acorns. • Although some acorns are bitter, others are sweet and are often boiled and eaten by the people of southern Europe. The American Indians crushed the nuts, washed them to remove the bitter taste, ground them into a meal, and flattened them into cakes, which they cooked and ate. • Wood from this tree is slow to rot and was the most desired material for shipbuilding before steel. The oak wood of the Shrine of Edward at Westminster Abbey is still sound today after 900 years. • The largest known oak is in Gloucestershire, England. It is 15 metres (48 feet) around.

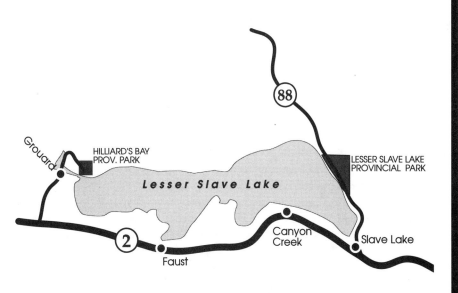

Slave Lake to Grouard

SLAVE LAKE

Originally named Sawridge, the town of Slave Lake was founded on the northeast shore of Lesser Slave Lake at the beginning of the century. It was an important centre for steamboats that crossed the lake, gold rushers, and Peace River homesteaders. In 1935-36, the lake flooded the town and the residents relocated to the present site.

North of Slave Lake on Highway #88 is the Lesser Slave Lake Provincial Park. The campground itself is on a ridge about four metres (13 feet) above the lake. You can reach the long beach by way of three sets of stairs leading from the higher ground.

Lesser Slave Lake Provincial Park

The high hill you see as you drive north to the park is Marten's Mountain. The gravel road to the lookout tower on the mountain is steep, with many sharp turns. Those pulling a trailer should leave it in the parking lot below. Once at the top, you get a panoramic view of Lesser Slave Lake and the surrounding area.

If you feel energetic and want to see a scenic, back country lake, hike the Lily Lake Trail. The path is three kilometres (1.8 miles), with an elevation of 1,024 metres (3,328 feet) at the beginning and 905 metres (2,942 feet) at the lake. By contrast, Lesser Slave Lake elevation is 576 metres (1,872 feet).

Because of the mountain's height and cooler climate, lodgepole pine, balsam fir, devil's club, ostrich fern, and five-leaved creeping raspberry are found on the slopes. These normally inhabit the foothills regions.

Marten's Mountain is the site of Alberta's first forest fire lookout tower. It is the oldest, continually-managed fire tower in Alberta. The metal structure at the summit was built in 1956 to replace the original wooden one, erected in 1923.

During the summer months, a golden pike/golden walleye fishing derby is held on Lesser Slave Lake. Weekly prizes are awarded, so enter whenever you arrive. If you prefer a more artistic endeavour, Devonshire Beach at the south end of the park is the scene of the Alberta Open Sandcastle Competition on the Canada Day long weekend. Prizes of up to $800 are offered in the three-category contest.

Get your children up early on the day of the sandcastle competition so they can take part in the treasure hunt. On the night before, pirates from Dog Island creep ashore and bury treasure in the sand. Parents are allowed to help with the clues.

Steps to beach, Lesser Slave Lake Provincial Park

If building isn't your talent, grab three other people, making sure one of you is female, and enter the beach volleyball championship, also held at Devonshire. The game is played according to beach volleyball rules and the net is men's regulation height. First prize is 50 per cent of the proceeds, plus medals.

For winter fun there is the Grizzly Ridge ski hill, cross-country skiing at the provincial park, and snowmobiling. For those not wanting to wander too far from town, try the Sawridge Creek Trail — a two kilometre (1.2 mile) cross-country path through the town of Slave Lake.

CANYON CREEK, KINUSO, AND FAUST

The only hotel on Alberta's second largest lake is at Canyon Creek. The building was originally constructed as a fish hatchery in the 1920s, when fish were the main food for mink raised on ranches in the area. At the end of this period, the hatchery was converted into a hotel.

Canyon Creek also has a marina, a campground, boat rentals, and a long beach. The town sponsors a sailing regatta on the August long weekend and you can drop in at the marina to weigh your catch for the golden pike/golden walleye competition.

Stop in at the Kinuso museum to see the 64th largest grizzly bear in the world. The bear was 19 years old when it was shot in 1981 and has a standing height of 2.4 metres (seven feet nine inches). The hide measures 2.7 metres (eight feet, nine inches) from the tip of the nose to the tip of the tail.

During the heavy shelling of London, England in the Second World War, St. Paul's Cathedral was damaged by a bomb. A piece of glass was recovered from the debris and brought to northern Alberta after the war. Drive into Faust and visit the St. Paul's Anglican Church. In the third window on the west side of the church is that piece of glass, safe behind a protective plastic covering.

St. Paul's Anglican Church, Faust

Grouard is one of the oldest communities in northern Alberta. Its mission was founded by Father Grouard in 1884. The work of art behind the altar in the church was painted by Grouard when he was a bishop.

The Grouard Campus of the Alberta Vocational Centre is located in the town. The Grouard Native Arts and Crafts Museum is in the Moosehorn Lodge Building at the centre. The exhibits feature Native works and you will see traditional costumes from various bands, Cree and Ojibwa birch bark canoes, birch bark scrolls circa 1840, an Ainu costume from the aboriginal Japanese people, and bead and porcupine quill work.

There are few exclusively Native museums like this in Western Canada and mobile displays have travelled to England, Germany, Japan, and Australia, as well as across Canada. If you are interested in Native arts, enroll in one of the workshops or short courses on fish scale art, caribou and moosehair tufting, and sand painting.

High Prairie to Girouxville

HIGH PRAIRIE

High Prairie takes wing with the annual Innisfail to High Prairie Classic Pigeon Race in August, sponsored by the High Prairie Racing Pigeon Club. The over 100 owners train their birds during the summer by taking them increasingly greater

distances, releasing them, and timing their flight home. Some entrants from as far away as Montreal and Port Hardy, B.C. arrive weeks ahead of the event to familiarize their pigeons with their new "home."

Early in the morning on race day the birds are released in Innisfail, south of Red Deer. They reach the finish line at Prairie Echo Hall north of High Prairie at about noon, after flying a distance of about 450 kilometres (280 miles). Some of the birds have been clocked at 65 km/h (40 mph).

Winagami Lake Provincial Park

Other activities of the day include horseshoes, baseball, and kids' games. In the evening an awards dinner and social are held.

From High Prairie take Highway #749 north to #679 and turn west to Winagami Provincial Park. The park has a rock causeway stretching out from the beach, a wide expanse of grass planted with ornamental trees and shrubs, and a boat launch. The lake has great fishing for walleye, perch, and pike.

McLENNAN

Continue west on Highway #679 to Highway #49 then turn north to McLennan, home of Hollandia Bakery, the largest, privately owned bakery in northern Alberta. Besides supplying baked goods in Alberta, they also cover the North West Territories and the Yukon. Tours can be arranged by phoning 324-3582.

Kimiwan Lake is the intersection of three major bird flyways: the Mississippi, Pacific, and Central. 27,000 shorebirds rest here on their yearly migrations. Many beautiful waterfowl nest on its shores and the lake is a protected wildlife breeding area. Visit the interpretive centre or wander along the boardwalk and see how many species you can recognize of the more than 200 that frequent the area. Especially watch for snowy owls, bald eagles, and whistling swans.

Kimiwan is shallow, but has good fishing for perch, walleye, and pike.

The Cost of Ingenuity

McLennan owes its existence to the "ingenuity" of an Edmonton, Dunvegan, and British Columbia (ED&BC) Railway employee, Hughie Hunter. The railroad was searching for a source of pure water for their steam locomotives and Hunter was sent from Grouard to Winagami Lake and Round Lake (Lake Kimiwan) to collect water for testing in Edmonton. • When he arrived back at Lesser Slave Lake, the water container was empty and rather than retrace his steps for another sample, he dipped the vessel into these waters. The water received high marks from the chemist in Edmonton. Thanks to his resourcefulness, the railway spent years hauling water from Lesser Slave Lake to McLennan, because the actual water from Winagami and Round Lakes ultimately proved unsuitable.

Donnelly, Falher, and Girouxville

DONNELLY

Set the first weekend of August aside and attend the annual Smoky River Agriculture Society Fair, an event that has been a tradition in the area since 1934. One of the special features you will be interested in is the Antique and Vintage Tractor Pull, where contending tractors pull a weight transferring machine over a measured distance. The tractors must have been built before 1959, with rubber tires or steel wheels, and they must be single tires only. A prize is also awarded for the best looking tractor.

Alfalfa processing plant, Falher

Tables are laden with hundreds of entries in the home cooking contest, the handicraft competitions, the plant and flower displays, the pioneer skills, and many other categories. Take part in the pancake breakfasts, watch the parade and the gymkhana events, have fun at the midway, or dance the night away. There is much to keep you entertained.

Falher is on Highway #49, west of Highway #2, and is called "Honey Capital of Canada." The world's largest bee is on Third Avenue and Rue Principale in a small park. The insect is a monument to honey producers in the district who extract more than 2.5 million kilograms (5 million pounds) of honey annually. Take a tour of one of the honey extracting plants, but be careful what you touch; everything is sticky, including the door handles.

That smell in the air is from two alfalfa pellet processing plants located in Falher. Large trucks haul green alfalfa leaves and stems to the plant and dump them in an immense pile in front. A front-end loader picks up the alfalfa and deposits it in a rotating drum, where it is dehydrated by 540° C (1000° F) heat. The dried alfalfa is then pressed into pellets.

The processing plants are at the east end of town. Park across the road and watch the process. In the evening, the raging fires in the heaters can be clearly seen from outside.

Grotto, Girouxville Museum

Girouxville is three kilometres (1.8 miles) north of Highway #49 on #744. The Girouxville Museum is one of the best in the North. Behind the wrought iron wheel gate, on main street just past the Co-op, are two totem poles, the blue museum building, a large windmill, and antique machinery.

Inside the museum, alcoves contain complete scenes from the past — you can even look into a trapper's cabin and see how it was furnished one hundred years ago. Two stairways lead to a second level with its numerous showcases. All the wall space is taken up with paintings and artifacts.

Drive back to Highway #2 and head north. There are many old buildings along this highway. One of them, a small, log house about 14 kilometres (8.5 miles) north on the west side, is called Moonshine Cabin by the residents of the area. Years ago, two brothers built this cabin, then used it as base for their still and moonshine operation.

Peace River and District

During the 1930s, the people of the Peace River area were desperate for a railroad to be constructed from northern Alberta to the B.C. coast. When their request was refused by the government and the railroad, they held meetings to discuss ceding from Alberta and creating their own country. Eventually, they calmed down and decided to remain as part of the province. Because of those meetings, however, northern Alberta is not referred to as the Peace District or the Peace Region, but the Peace Country.

PEACE RIVER

The drive into the Peace River Valley is one of the most beautiful you will take. The road is long and winding, with rolling hills on one side and glimpses of the Heart Valley on the other.

Most people have heard the story of Twelve Foot Davis and how he noticed that two claims at the Cariboo gold rush in British Columbia had been improperly staked. He measured them and claimed the twelve foot wide strip between them. It is estimated that he made between $12,000 and $20,000 from that discovery.

Twelve Foot Davis

Few people know how Davis occupied himself when he retired from mining. He headed north and set up a string of trading posts in the Peace River area, in competition with the Hudson's Bay Company. It was a hard life being a free trader in the Company's territory and over time he grew to hate the Company. • Davis liked to spend hours on a hill overlooking the Smoky, Peace, and Heart Rivers and he told his friend Peace River Jim Cornwall that one of his wishes was to be buried on top of that hill. • Davis died in Grouard, Alberta, in 1900, and was buried there. But Cornwall, remembering his wish, petitioned to have him reburied at Peace River. Because of red tape, it took him ten years to finally accomplish his friend's last wish. At the same time, he fulfilled Davis' other wish — to be buried with his feet pointing downhill — "So I can piss on the Hudson's Bay Company."

Peace River and Town

To find Davis' grave, drive east on 100th Avenue, which heads southeast after passing the United Church. The road, dug into the side of the hill, climbs and curves its way to the summit. Sections of the roadway have begun to fall away, so drive carefully. From the crest of the hill, look out over the Peace and Smoky Rivers, the town, and the hills of the Peace River below you. .

The town of Peace River is the finish line of the Jet Boat Races which begin at Grande Cache on the Smoky River. This is one of the many races that make up the World River Boat Racing Championship.

Take a cruise on the river in a sternwheeler. If speed is what you like, tour the river to Tar Island in a jet boat, stay the night, and arrive back the next day.

While there, watch for the magic dancing flames on the water. At low water, natural gas leaks from the ground and rises on the river. When lit, it makes a colourful and unique picture.

Hiking trails weave through and around the town. You can stroll along the river bank or through the historic downtown section. There is fishing for goldeye, northern pike, chub, and pickerel, but you had better take some chest waders along.

For winter fun, try the Peace River Ski Hill on Misery Mountain. If you are in town on St. Patrick's Day, take in the annual St. Patrick's Day Pig Race, where teams of two men race their pigs down the main street. This has been a popular sport in Peace River for decades and photos of this race date back to 1906.

SHAFTESBURY TRAIL

Reverend J. Gough Brick, an Anglican missionary, established the Shaftesbury mission near Peace River in 1887. He taught the Métis to grow grain and vegetables and soon a colony, the Shaftesbury Settlement, grew up around the mission.

Reverend Brick's sample of Red Fife wheat gained international prominence at the Columbian Exposition in Chicago in 1896, and the Peace Country began its reign as one of the best grain growing areas in Canada.

The Shaftesbury Trail was used by Natives, fur traders, explorers, missionaries, and Klondikers. The huge monument on the east side the trail (Highway #684), is the Mackenzie Cairn.

Alexander Mackenzie spent the winter of 1792-93 at Fort Fork on the bank of the Peace River, just south of the present-day town. He and nine companions left the fort in May, 1793 to attempt the first overland expedition to the Pacific Ocean. They reached it in July of that year.

For 62 years, the St. Augustine Mission was a day and boarding school for white, Métis, and Native children. The only remains of the mission—a small church, a cairn to the mission, and some graves — are in a small yard surrounded by a fence.

Located on land where the mission once stood is the Peace River Correctional Centre. If you wish to enter the yard to see the church and graves, you have to ask permission at the correctional centre's office.

Shaftesbury Trail

Continue on the Shaftesbury Trail beside the river until it forks, about 20 kilometres (12 miles) south of Peace River. The left fork will lead you down to the river and the Shaftesbury Ferry; the other will take you out of the valley and to Highway #2 south of Grimshaw.

There is a Native legend that whoever drinks from the Peace River will always come back. There is a fountain at the tourist information booth in the town of Peace River. If you fell in love with this country, drink the water to ensure that you, too, will return.

Chapter 6
Fairview to Hythe

This parcel of northern boreal parkland is within Peace River Country, which stretches over the Alberta border into British Columbia.

Just west of Rycroft is Nardam, a 3.6 hectare (nine acre) man-made campground with a rainbow trout stocked pond (no power boats allowed), playground, kitchen, camping stalls, and potable water.

To get to Moonshine Lake Provincial Park, go 29 kilometres (18 miles) west of Spirit River on Highway #49, then five kilometres (three miles) north on #725. The rainbow trout bite best in late evening and the running water at the fish cleaning table makes filleting them easy.

About 10 kilometres (six miles) north of Sexsmith are the Burnt River Hills. Deer, moose, and elk hunting is good here. The area is also a flyway for geese and ducks.

Kleskun Hills are 20 kilometres (12 miles) east of Grande Prairie on Highway #34, three kilometres (1.8 miles) north, then one kilometre west. They are the remnants of a 70-million-year-old river delta. Remains of dinosaurs and marine life have been discovered in these ancient hills.

Two kilometres northwest of Beaverlodge along Highway #2 is the South Peace Centennial Museum. Fifteen buildings brim with displays, while 35 gas and diesel tractors, 20 antique cars and trucks, and six steam traction engines decorate the grounds.

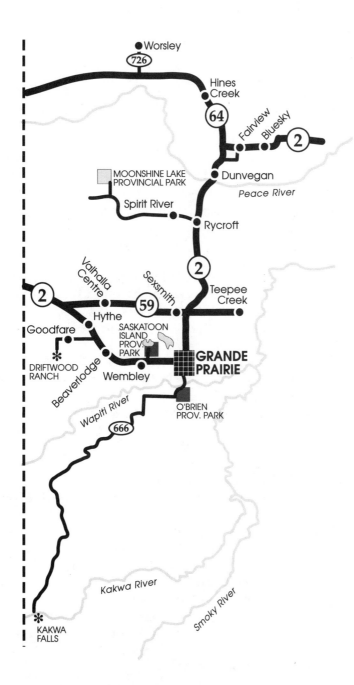

Fairview to Spirit River

FAIRVIEW

Early settlers travelling along the Dunvegan Trail found water at Boucher Creek and named the settlement Waterhole. Pioneers arrived to claim the land and soon a community was established to serve the area. By the time the Central Canada Railway line went through 6.5 kilometres (four miles) to the north in 1928, Waterhole was a thriving village with a hospital, churches, hotels, and banks. But 1928 was Waterhole's final year. Since growing businesses preferred being near the railway, the merchants of Waterhole relocated to the new hamlet of Fairview.

Fairview College opened its doors in November 1951 and, at the time, was known as the Fairview School of Agriculture and Home Economics. Fire destroyed much of the campus in 1958, but it was quickly rebuilt and has been enlarged since.

In 1968, a new women's residence, the Plant Sciences building, and the Animal Sciences building were introduced. Western Canada's only Animal Health Technology project began here in 1974.

The school became Fairview College in 1978. It continues to offer northern residents a varied curriculum, including the only turf grass management program in Western Canada, Canada's first Harley-Davidson technician course, and a world famous beekeeping program.

Despite its name — RCMP Museum — Fairview's museum is not an RCMP museum. It is located in the house formerly occupied by an RCMP officer.

BLUESKY, HINES CREEK, AND WORSLEY

Bluesky is ten kilometres (six miles) east of Fairview. The hamlet was featured on the back of the old Canadian dollar bill.

North of Fairview is Hines Creek. Visit the End of Steel Heritage Museum, with its historic buildings and refurbished Northern Alberta Railway caboose. A church, constructed in the 1930s, has been restored and is available for special occasions like baptisms, reunions, or anniversaries.

After touring the museum, have a picnic at one of the tables, play a game of horseshoes, or try a round of golf at the Hines Creek Golf Club. Many of the lakes between Hines Creek and the B.C. border are popular fishing holes.

For downhill and cross-country skiers, Whispering Pines Ski Hill is 25 kilometres (15.5 miles) northwest of Worsley.

DUNVEGAN

South of Fairview is the historic site of Dunvegan. Dunvegan is set in the valley of the Peace River and the view during the winding drive down through the hills is magnificent.

As you near the bottom of the hill, you will see the Dunvegan Bridge. At 550 metres (1,800 feet), it is the longest suspension bridge in Alberta and the fourth longest in Canada. It is also the only suspension bridge for vehicles in Alberta.

St. Charles Mission, Dunvegan

The entrance to the historic site is at the last curve before the bridge. There is a picnic area and camping for those who wish to stay a few days. To the east is the Dunvegan Market Garden, where you can buy fresh vegetables grown in soil that was first cultivated almost 200 years ago.

Established on the Peace River in 1805 by Archibald McLeod of the North West Company, the initial Fort Dunvegan was situated west of the present site. It was named after McLeod's ancestral home on the Isle of Skye, off the west coast of Scotland.

The Hudson's Bay Company assumed charge of the post when the two companies amalgamated in 1821, and in 1887-88 the Company decided a second fort was needed. The factor's house was the first building erected.

The first permanent mission wasn't constructed until 1866, despite the fact that the Catholic Church had been sending priests to the area for over 20 years. It was called the St. Charles Mission and it was built by Father Christopher Tissier at Fort Dunvegan.

Obtain a map of the site and take the self-guided walking tour. The St. Charles Mission Rectory, built in 1889, and the St. Charles Mission Church, dedicated in 1885, overlook the Peace River beside the campgrounds. At the church, you can view historical displays, inspect a model of the site, and laugh at a puppet play.

After leaving the grounds, turn left and follow the gravel road under the bridge. You will pass the Bridge View market garden, full of fruits, vegetables, and hamburgers for the really hungry.

"The Maples," Dunvegan

Beside the market garden is an old structure, almost hidden in the trees. Look at it closely, for this is the factor's house from the second fort. It is the only building left from the fur trade era.

Continue on the road past the cairn dedicated to the original Dunvegan settlement and you will arrive at "The Maples." The tall, broad, Manitoba maple trees shade tables and fire pits along the Peace River.

To the north of the parking lot is an asphalt walkway through the trees. There are benches on which to pause and enjoy the peace and quiet of the forest. Children will love this walk— there is a playground at the end.

Manitoba Maples

A small cairn, dedicated to St. Saviour's Anglican Mission, sits beside the parking lot. It has the following inscription: *These Manitoba Maples mark the site of St. Saviour's Mission to the Beaver Indians. Established in 1879 by Thomas W. Bunn. Resident missionaries Rev. John Gouch Brick 1882-1886 and Rev. Alfred Campbell Garrioch 1886-1891 extensively promoted local agriculture and served the mission successfully until it was closed in 1891. The seeds planted by Rev A. Garrioch before his departure flourished and gave this place its name — The Maples.* One of Garrioch's daughters, Caroline, is buried in the bush beside "The Maples." Follow the faint path to the east of the cairn and you will find her small, solitary grave enclosed by a white picket fence. She was only two days old.

SPIRIT RIVER AND RYCROFT

At one time, Rycroft and Spirit River were one community. A small trading post was established on both banks of the Chepe Sepe ("Ghost River" in Cree) in 1891. The current townsite was surveyed in 1915. When the railroad went through, Spirit River remained and Rycroft moved to the railway line.

Just west of Rycroft is Nardam, a 3.6 hectare (nine acre) man-made campground with a rainbow trout stocked pond (no power boats allowed), playground, kitchen, camping stalls, and potable water.

Moonshine Lake Provincial Park

To get to Moonshine Lake Provincial Park, go 29 kilometres (18 miles) west of Spirit River on Highway #49, then five kilometres (three miles) north on #725. The rainbow trout bite best in late evening and the running water at the fish cleaning table makes filleting them easy.

Called Mirage Lake up until prohibition, the lake's name was changed to Moonshine Lake by a Métis who, during the years of the liquor ban, had apparatus for distilling liquor erected in many locations nearby.

Sexsmith to Grande Prairie

SEXSMITH

Sexsmith is 46 kilometres (28 miles) south of Rycroft. The old blacksmith shop has been reconditioned and is now a museum. Most of the antique tools and equipment were catalogued during restoration and returned to their original places in the shop. The changing role of the smith through the years is shown through the collection of tools on display.

Ask about the location of the hollowed out logs, where the smith kept his supply of illegal liquor hidden from the prying eyes of the NWMP.

Sexsmith Museum

About 10 kilometres (six miles) north of Sexsmith are the Burnt River Hills. Deer, moose, and elk hunting is good here. The area is also a flyway for geese and ducks.

To see Alberta's only straw church, turn east onto Highway #674 and drive to Tee-pee Creek, famous for staging Canada's largest amateur stampede. Just past the hamlet at Highway #733, turn north, drive 13 kilometres (eight miles) and turn east. Go six kilometres (3.7 miles) to a stop sign and turn south for about 3/4 of a kilometre. You will see a large white hall and a small, stucco building on the west side of the road.

When first constructed in 1957, the church was constructed from flax straw bales assembled to form the structure. After a year of services in the remarkable little building, the bales were covered with green and white stucco on the outside and plywood on the inside. Though it hasn't been used for many years, it is still referred to as the Straw Church by the residents of the area.

VALHALLA CENTRE

The first Scandinavians came north in 1911 and settled west of Sexsmith. They were joined the next year by more immigrants from their homeland. The settlers, wanting some reminder of the country they had left behind, named their district Valhalla Centre after the great hall of the dead heros of Norse mythology. The creamery they established in 1920 won first prize in a Dominion-wide butter making competition in 1923.

GRANDE PRAIRIE

Until 1916, Lake Saskatoon was the distribution centre for this region of the North. In that year, the railway made Grande Prairie, originally called Buffalo Plains, the end of the line, and most businesses abandoned Lake Saskatoon for the new town.

Visit Muskoseepi Park in the middle of Grande Prairie. It has over 400 hectares (1,000 acres) of parkland along the Bear Creek Valley and around Crystal Lake, which is a bird sanctuary located in the northeast corner of the city.

Bear Creek ripples through Grande Prairie. The Muskoseepi Park Pavilion is at one extremity of the creek while the Bear Creek South picnic centre is at the other. They are linked by the Bear Creek Corridor, with its hiking and bicycling trails, a wilderness area, a reservoir, and a lake.

Centennial Park is the "heart" of the woodlands, with its fishing and skating pond, Pioneer Museum, mini golf, lawn bowling, horseshoe pits, and amphitheatre. Look for the stuffed grizzly bear and the stuffed albino moose in the wildlife section of the museum.

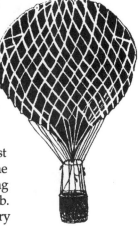

The Prairie Gallery, at 10209 - 99th Street, displays works by local artists, has exhibits from other locales, and offers art classes, lectures, and seminars for those interested in the arts.

Lewis Brothers, the world's northern-most winery, is located in Grande Prairie. Some of their wine originates from the blending of honey, saskatoon berries, and rhubarb. Phone 532-WINE for a tour of the winery and to procure a bottle of their unique creation.

Hot air balloon

Imagine the sight of 20 or more colourful, hot air balloons rising slowly into the blue sky, then visualize the scene repeating itself day after day. That is what happened in Grande Prairie in 1979 when the city hosted the first annual Canadian Hot Air Balloon Championships. It occurred again in 1989, when the 10th annual meet was held in the city. In the years between, Grande Prairie presented other ballooning events and championships and it is now known as the "Hot Air Balloon Capital of Canada."

Adventurous travellers might want to try a trip to the Kakwa Falls in Wild Kakwa Wilderness Park. The falls are near the Alberta/British Columbia border, southwest of Grande Prairie, and you can drive (four-wheel, that is) as far as the campground. You then have to hike the remaining distance of about 32 kilometres (20 miles). The falls are 27 metres (90 feet) high and the gorge is 60 metres (195 feet) wide and four kilometres (2.5 miles) long. About 400 metres (1,300 feet) further downstream from the Kakwa is another, smaller waterfall.

Kleskun Hills are 20 kilometres (12 miles) east of Grande Prairie on Highway #34, three kilometres (1.8 miles) north, then one kilometre west. They are the remnants of a 70-million-year-old river delta. Remains of dinosaurs and marine life have been discovered in these ancient hills.

Trumpeter Swan

The Trumpeter Swan is the largest waterfowl in the world. It weighs between 11.4 and 16 kilograms (25 to 35 pounds) and has a wing span of 2.5 to 3 metres (8 to 10 feet). If stretched out, it could stand as tall as 1.2 metres (4 feet) and be 1.5 metres (5 feet) in length from bill to tail. • The largest breeding ground in Canada for these majestic birds is in the Grande Prairie district. If you want to see them, try Little Lake in Saskatoon Island Provincial Park or one of these other lakes: Henderson, Flying Shot, Buffalo, or Gummer. Check at the Muskoseepi Park Pavilion for more information.

Wembley to Hythe

WEMBLEY

In 1924, the railway extended 24 kilometres (15 miles) west from Grande Prairie. The balance of the town of Lake Saskatoon moved to the line and changed its name to Wembley.

Between 1926 and 1932, Herman Trelle, who farmed near Wembley, won 135 world-wide awards at the Chicago International Hay and Grain Show for grains he had grown. Beginning in 1926, he swept the Grand Championship for Hard Red Spring wheat three years in a row. He also won the World Wheat Championship that year, and was crowned Wheat King of the

World. It was the first time in Chicago World's Fair history that both championships had been awarded to the same person.

For palaeontologists, dinosaur remains have been found at Pipestone Creek Park, near Wembley.

Alex Monkman

Alex Monkman was a jack-of-all-trades. In 1899, as a fur trader, he built a house and set up a store at Saskatoon Lake. He tried a little farming and in 1906 he began ranching. He bought a herd of cattle and developed it into 150 head before having to relinquish the land in 1908 to homesteaders. He then returned to farming and started trapping. • Monkman also liked to explore. He discovered a pass from Beaverlodge through the Rockies to Prince George, B.C. But the railways weren't interested in establishing a line there and the Alberta government refused to build a highway through the pass. The residents of the area decided to construct their own road. They were promised funding to improve it by the Edmonton Chamber of Commerce, but not until they could drive a car over their route. • On September 3, 1938, a Model-T and driver started across the partially completed trail to Harisard, British Columbia. Late supplies, bad weather, and the freezing of the Herick River, forced the suspension of the trek for the winter. • Support money was slow in coming in 1939, after the outbreak of the Second World War. Within a few months, the car and the idea were totally abandoned. • In 1967, the Grande Prairie River Rats Association located the old car, loaded it onto five jet boats, ferried it to Prince George, and then hauled it to Grand Prairie. The car has been restored and can be seen in the museum in Grande Prairie. The Alex Monkman Highway, however, is still just a dream.

BEAVERLODGE

The Pioneer campsite at Beaverlodge is dedicated to the enjoyment of residents and visitors. The Lower Beaverlodge School, built in 1912, is used as a tourist information booth. A teacher, and a desk and other items help preserve the old school atmosphere.

Lower Beaverlodge School, 1912

Visit the Beaverlodge Museum Tavern in the Beaverlodge Hotel. Before entering, do a little window shopping. One window displays a bear, another guns, while others have birds, wagon wheels, and old carts. Inside, the tavern is laid out like a museum, with stuffed animals, historic artifacts and exhibits. After your tour, stop in at the Steak Pit for some delicious buffalo burgers.

Canada's most northern Agricultural Research Station is at Beaverlodge. It was organized to breed new strains of barley, canola, and wheat and to work on soil fertility, weed control, and the study and breeding of bees.

Beaverlodge

Two kilometres northwest of Beaverlodge along Highway #2 is the South Peace Centennial Museum. Fifteen buildings brim with displays, while 35 gas and diesel tractors, 20 antique cars and trucks, and six steam traction engines decorate the grounds.

Try to be there on the third Sunday in July, when Pioneer Days are held and much of the machinery is put into operation. A tractor parade is followed by demonstrations of shingle sawing, silage cutting, steam threshing, and log sawing. This is one of the largest operating museums in Alberta, and expansion plans are being developed.

GOODFARE

Some of the unusual birds and animals at the Driftwood Ranch are Vietnamese pot-bellied pigs, African pygmy goats, African Ankole cattle, Chinese geese, and Japanese snow monkeys. One of the animals you don't want to miss is the Joose. Its father was a moose, and its mother was a Jersey cow.

Two of the jaguars raised here were used in the movie *Bird On A Wire* starring Mel Gibson and Goldie Hawn. The Siberian tiger in the fight scene near the end of the movie was also from this ranch.

Driftwood Ranch, Goodfare

Driftwood Ranch is on Highway #671 at the end of the paved road west of Goodfare. Because the animals are wild, you can only view the site on a guided tour. Try to call ahead because the farm is closed to the public when field work needs to be done.

HYTHE

Back on Highway #2 turn west and drive to Hythe. The town was nicknamed the "Town of Flowing Wells" because it is sitting on a huge underground water supply. The tourist information booth is in a 1910 Tack Shop.

Because of the abundance of saskatoons in the area, many residents grow them commercially. The South Peace Fruit Growers Association has built a plant on the west side of Hythe to process these berries. From Hythe you can travel west into British Columbia, or take Highway #59 back to Sexsmith.

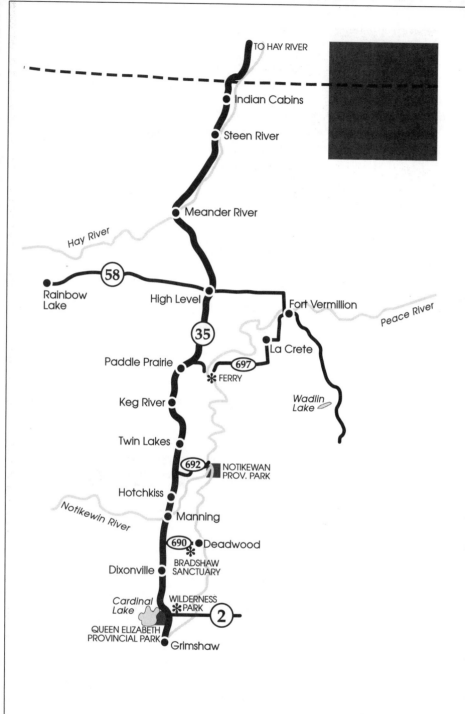

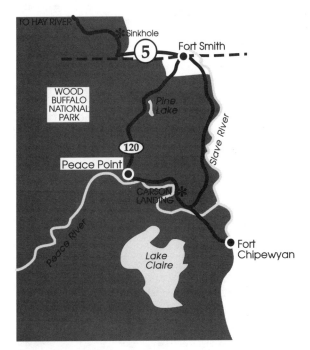

Chapter 7
Mackenzie Highway

Along the Mackenzie Highway, farms with decorated yards, creeks, ponds, and green and yellow crops alternate with long stretches of trees. If you like honey, many farmers have this sweet foodstuff for sale.

Alexander Mackenzie

On June 3rd, 1789, Alexander Mackenzie left Fort Chipewyan on his first attempt to locate a passage to the Pacific Ocean. He travelled down the Slave River to Great Slave Lake, discovered a river running west, and followed it. The river eventually turned north and after days of paddling, Mackenzie found himself staring at an unbroken landscape of ice. He had reached the Arctic Ocean. • Disappointed, he returned to Fort Chipewyan. It had taken him 102 days to travel 3,323 kilometres (2,060 miles) to the mouth and back of the largest river in Canada and the second longest river in North America. It was named the Mackenzie River in his honour. • Alexander Mackenzie departed Fort Chipewyan in the fall of 1792 in a second attempt at reaching the Pacific Ocean. He and his companions spent the winter at Fort Fork on the Peace River and continued their journey in May, 1793. They canoed down rivers and portaged across land until they reached the Pacific Ocean on their 74th day. The return to Fort Chipewyan took only 33 days. • Mackenzie, who had left eastern Canada for Fort Chipewyan in the summer of 1792, was the first European to travel across the North American continent north of Mexico.

Grimshaw to Paddle Prairie

GRIMSHAW

A cairn at the north end of Grimshaw marks the town as Mile Zero of the Mackenzie Highway. Before you begin your journey, though, spend an afternoon at the Wilderness Park. It is just a few kilometres east on Highway #2 and is sponsored by the Grimshaw Agricultural Society.

At the parking lot is a map of the area showing two ponds, walking paths, cross-country skiing routes, and wheelchair accessible trails. The first pond is stocked with trout, the second with grayling. Docks extend out into the water and there are picnic tables set throughout the park.

Mile Zero Cairn, Grimshaw

Queen Elizabeth Provincial Park is northwest of Grimshaw. The queen dedicated the park in 1978 while on a visit to Alberta. A plaque on a large rock near the entrance commemorates that day.

DIXONVILLE

As you drive into Dixonville, watch for Max's Trading Post and Museum, a small log building on the north side of the road. A cook stove stands in the centre of the room. Shelves full of antiques, lamps hanging from the ceiling, and old comics are just some of the articles you will see.

Dixonville is famous for its annual craft sale, held the first weekend in December. Everyone is welcome and craftspeople and buyers arrive from across northern Alberta to participate in the sale.

One of the two churches in Dixonville is Strang Presbyterian. Dr. Margaret Strang arrived in the area around 1930. Her practice, first established in North Star then moved to Dixonville, covered an area of about 1,550 square kilometres (600 square miles). To tend to her patients, Dr. Strang travelled by horseback.

Dr. Strang was also a minister, and the settlers built a church in Dixonville for Sunday services. When not out taking care of the sick, she assisted with the construction of the building. She married, and in the 1940s, Dr. Strang-Savage accepted a posting with the United Church of Canada and moved to Cold Lake.

DEADWOOD

If you want to observe quails, pheasants, swans, partridge, pigeons, doves, and wild turkeys in different stages of growth (three or four clutches of these birds are hatched during the

summer), turn east onto Highway #690 towards Deadwood. Drive 3.2 kilometres (two miles) then turn south and travel 1.6 kilometres (one mile) to the Bradshaw Bird Sanctuary, a privately owned reserve.

Many exotic birds are raised in movable pens in the yard. If you are quiet and careful, you may enter the pens to take pictures.

Bradshaw Bird Sanctuary

The owners have excavated two swimming ponds for swans and geese, with islands in the centre for them to relax on. Ask about the two friendly trumpeter swans that emerge from the water to eat bread out of your hand.

Trumpeter Swans, Bradshaw Bird Sanctuary

At the end of the tour, you will be invited into a small cabin where you may sign the guest register. You will also get a peacock feather, and have the opportunity to see the many artistic crafts that can be created with the birds' feathers. The handiwork is entered in the Dixonville Craft Show every year.

NORTH STAR

The Charles Plavin homestead is located three kilometres (1.8 miles) south of North Star on the old Highway #35. Plavin, originally from Latvia, began homesteading in the Peace Country around 1918. On his land, he constructed two log homes: one has

home-made beds and central heating while the other has a fireplace and sauna. Both still stand and, although the doors are locked, you can walk through the yard and inspect his workmanship.

Charles Plavin Homestead, south of Northstar

The Notikewin River drifts through Manning. You must descend into the valley to reach the town. Manning was known as Aurora until 1947, when it was renamed after the Hon. E.C. Manning, then Premier of Alberta. Some of the businesses in town, though, still use Aurora in their names.

Inside the Battle River Museum are an antique wrench display, a dairy exhibit, stuffed animals, mounted heads, a large arrangement of farm machinery, and a beautifully sculptured, old-fashioned cash register.

In 1987, Manning was named the official headquarters of the "Land of the Mighty Moose." Hunters from Alberta, the rest of Canada, and the United States come to partake in some of the best moose hunting in Alberta. The Manning district is also establishing itself as a centre for bow hunting, especially during deer season.

If hunting is not for you, try downhill skiing at the Manning Ski Hill, northeast of town, or go cross-country skiing on one of the trails.

HOTCHKISS AND NOTIKEWIN PROVINCIAL PARK

The Condy Meadows Golf course is near Hotchkiss. Just north of Hotchkiss is a long, slow hill into the Meikle River valley — a nice break from the previous stretches of farmland.

Notikewin River

To fish the Peace River, head 21 kilometres (13 miles) north of Hotchkiss, then east on Highway #692 to Notikewin Provincial Park. The road into the park is steep and winding and very dangerous when wet. The boat launch is on the Peace River and the picnic area overlooks the merging of the Notikewin and the Peace. If you hike to the end of the camping area and walk through the bush, you will come to the Notikewin River, a small but scenic estuary.

On an island in the Peace River near here is a grove of 200-year-old white spruce. A stand of ostrich fern up to 2 metres (6.5 feet.) tall is on an island in the Notikewin River.

Notikewin River

The Notikewin River was known by the Natives as the First Battle River because it was the site of a clash between two hostile tribes. The river running beside the Condy Meadows Golf Course was called the Second Battle River. Its name has since been changed to the Hotchkiss River. Another stream in the area is known as the Third Battle River.

Twin Lakes has a service station and restaurant. Judging by the number of large trucks often in the parking lot, the food must be delicious here.

If you are hot and sweaty and want to stop to cool off, turn west onto the gravel road at Twin Lakes and drive to the recreation area. The lake is great for swimming and is stocked with rainbow trout. Gas powered boats are not allowed on the water.

Keg River has a service station, confectionery, and post office.

Paddle Prairie is a Métis settlement with a service station and the Ghostkeeper's Store. For those heading to Fort Vermilion, the Paddle Prairie ferry crosses the Peace River at Tompkins Landing, about 10 kilometres (six miles) north and 10 kilometres east of Paddle Prairie on Highway #697. The gravel road on the other side of the river leads to La Crete, a Mennonite village south of Fort Vermilion.

If you are travelling Highway #35 at night, especially in the winter, watch for the aurora borealis (northern lights). The luminous rippling bands can be seen about 300 nights a year in this area and this is the best road from which to view them. Southwest of a line between Peace River and Edmonton, the number of sightings drop to approximately 160 a year and in the south they only appear about 30 nights a year.

High Level to Indian Cabins

High Level

High Level is at Kilometre 298 (Mile 180) on the Mackenzie Highway and is part of the Peace River Country. Although only slightly more than 160,000 hectares (400,000 acres) are settled this far north, there are millions more hectares waiting to be opened. The three grain elevators in the town are the most northerly in the world and handle more than 2.5 million bushels of grain each year.

Mural, High Level

High Level is in the Footner Lakes Forest region. The forest is larger than New Brunswick and includes seven of the 17 ecological districts in the province. The area is used for logging, oil and gas exploration, hunting, trapping, fishing, recreation, and by naturalists. Most of the forest is not accessible by road so much of its flora and fauna are never seen or spoiled.

Grain elevators, High Level

High Level has the largest saw mill in Alberta. It requires 96 truck loads of logs each day to remain in operation and produces about 240 million board feet of lumber a year.

If golf is your sport and you are in High Level around June 21, enter the annual Midnight Open Golf Tournament. It is held on the weekend closest to the longest day of the year, when the sun shines almost 24 hours.

FORT VERMILION

East of High Level on Highway #58 is Fort Vermilion. The town, on the Peace River, vies with Fort Chipewyan for being the oldest settlement in Alberta. Both were established in 1788 and both celebrated their bicentennial in 1988. The highway running south of Fort Vermilion to Slave Lake was renumbered from #67 to #88 to honour Fort Vermilion's 200th birthday.

The first post near present-day Fort Vermilion was called the Old Establishment. It was built by Charles Boyer of the North West Company in 1788 and was a few kilometres down stream from where the town is today. The location and name of the post changed

Bay Factor's House, Fort Vermillion

many times until, in 1830, the present site was chosen. The name Fort Vermilion, indicating the red clay deposits found in the river banks, was agreed upon that same year.

The Peace River was surveyed up to the Old Establishment by a government surveyor named Vaudrevil in 1789. This was the first recorded survey in Alberta.

Firewater

Over the years, liquor was often the most important commodity in the fur trade. Traders quickly realized the Natives' bartering skills were easily impaired by alcohol. • Because of the natives' low tolerance level, and to augment the supply, the men of the North West • Company diluted their liquor on a scale of thirty to seventy gallons of water to nine gallons of 132-proof rum and labeled the mixture High Wine. Hudson's Bay Company employees concocted English Brandy by adding iodine or tobacco juice to raw gin to give it an ochre shade, then thinning it with water. • The Natives soon caught on to the traders' tricks and began to test the alcohol given them by spitting a mouthful onto the fire. If the liquor was good, the flame would shoot up; if it was weak, the flame would die. This is the origin of the term "firewater."

By 1825, grain had been introduced in the Fort Vermilion region and small crops of barley were grown successfully. In 1876, wheat grown here won a gold medal at the World's Fair in Philadelphia.

A diphtheria epidemic at Fort Vermilion was prevented in January 1929 when "Wop" May, a World War I pilot and one of Canada's leading post-war bush pilots, and Vic Horner made a mercy flight to deliver an antitoxin to the village. They flew the 835 kilometres (517 miles) from Edmonton in an open cockpit Avro Avian aircraft, in temperatures as low as -35° C (-30° F).

Many old buildings still stand in Fort Vermilion and you can pick up a map to many of them at the tourist information booth. Look closely at the structure that houses the booth. It is a hand-hewn, dove-tailed log home, constructed in 1923.

If you need groceries, drop in at the Mary Batt and Son general store. Don't let the siding on the outside fool you. The Hudson's Bay Company Store, built in 1897, was dismantled in 1941 and its massive logs were used to construct this shop.

The Hudson's Bay factor's house was constructed in 1905 from locally sawn logs. It was declared a registered historic site in 1978.

Southeast of Fort Vermilion on Highway #88 is Wadlin Lake, one of the few pelican nesting grounds in Alberta. If you see the pelicans, do not excite them because they are on the endangered species list in Alberta. They are too sensitive to tolerate being harassed during breeding season and will desert their nest if even one person approaches the colony. Left without protection, the eggs and young birds, which have no feathers when hatched, are killed by heat, cold, or predators.

The Mackenzie Highway continues north from High Level and runs mainly through bush and muskeg. Meander River and Steen River are small communities.

The Hay River is a good fishing river. Don't be troubled by its colour; most of the rivers and creeks up north are brown from travelling through muskeg. Pike up to seven kilograms (15 pounds) and walleye to 4.5 kilograms (10 pounds) have been taken from this river.

Indian Cabins

Indian Cabins has a Native graveyard about 200 metres (650 feet) north of the hamlet's service station. It is surrounded by trees and populated by the infamous giant northern mosquito. Spirit houses cover the graves of children and adults.

Scaffold burial, Indian Cabins

Look up at a log supported in the branches of two trees. This is a scaffold burial, a traditional burial custom of some natives. A small baby was laid inside the hollowed out log and the coffin set in the limbs of the trees. It is the only surviving burial of this type in Alberta and is about 70 years old.

Wood Buffalo National Park

The Mackenzie Highway continues into the Northwest Territories, where it divides into numbered sections. To reach Wood Buffalo National Park in Alberta's north east, take Mackenzie Highway #5 to Fort Smith and then south to the park.

Wood Buffalo National Park, established in 1922, covers an area of 44,807 square kilometres (26,884 square miles). It is Canada's largest park and straddles the Alberta/Northwest Territories border. It was originally created to protect the country's last herd of wood buffalo, which then numbered less than 1,500.

About 6,600 plains bison were released in Wood Buffalo National Park shortly after it opened and the two species intermingled. The wood buffalo can be distinguished from the plains bison by their larger size and darker wool. The herd at the park is the largest free roaming collection of buffalo in the world.

Moose, caribou, black bears, wolves, and an abundance of smaller mammals (at least forty-six different types) range in the woodlands. Wood Buffalo also is one of the only nesting sites of the wild whooping crane in the world.

Sinkhole

While driving through the Northwest Territories section of the park, watch for the road leading to the Angus fire tower on the north side of the highway. Here you will see a sink-hole. This type of landscape is formed when running water, beneath the earth's surface, dissolves sedimentary rock and forms caves. The ceilings of the caves eventually collapse, producing round, deep, funnel-shaped cavities on the surface. Sometimes, a river will drop into a hole and travel underground for many metres before re-emerging. Pine Lake was formed by five collapsed sink-holes filled with water.

One of the world's largest inland deltas is partially within the park. The delta was formed by 10,000 years' worth of silt built-up from the Peace and Athabasca Rivers as they drained into the region.

Two hundred and fifty square kilometres (90 square miles) of the park is covered by salt water from salt springs that originate in a low escarpment. In a dry year, two metre (six feet) high mounds of salt may form at the springs.

There is a 36-site campground at Pine Lake, 66 kilometres (37 miles) south of Fort Smith. You can fish for eastern brook and rainbow trout in this lake, but you will need a park fishing license. Picnic areas and hiking trails abound, and tenting is allowed anywhere in the park.

Sinkhole, Wood Buffalo National Park

Because this is a wilderness park, the roads are gravel or sand. Depending how often they are used, they sometimes have grass growing between the tire lanes. The road from Fort Smith to Peace Point is good, and from Peace Point to Carlson landing is passable. If you are here in the winter, you can continue past Carlson Landing, south to Fort Chipewyan, since the road is designed for winter travelling. It is not advisable to travel through in the summer.

In the 18th century, warring Cree and Beaver signed a peace treaty at Peace Point, thus naming the river.

The Wood Buffalo Interpretive Centre, located in the Federal Building in Fort Smith, offers a variety of activities for visitors. There are slide presentations, hikes to the salt plains and Raup Lake, theatre, movies, and Native handicraft demonstrations. These events occur regularly throughout the summer.

Chapter 8
Namao to Newbrook

If you love history, this section of Alberta is for you. Railroad museums, historical trails, old buildings, and scientific research projects abound.

Drive about six kilometres (3.7 miles) south of Namao to the Alberta Pioneer Railway Museum. Walk through the yard and see old locomotives, railway cars, and many artifacts from the railroad history of western Canada. Some of the machinery dates back to 1877.

To see one of the best preserved buildings along the Athabasca Landing Trail, drive through Waugh and take the first turn west. Go about 1.6 kilometres (one mile) to the original St. Mary's Church, constructed beside the trail in 1905-07. It is the first Romanian Orthodox Church built in Alberta and the second in North America.

Between 1876 and 1903, Athabasca Landing was an important trading centre. It was the connection point between central and northern Alberta and was also the headquarters for northern missionaries of the Anglican Church. Druing the Klondike gold rush, many people camped at Athabasca Landing on their way over the all-Canadian route to the gold fields.

East of Athabasca, along Highway #55, is Amber Valley, the home of Alberta's first black settlers. In 1910, almost 200 blacks were led into the province by 22-year-old Jefferson Davis Edwards, and they settled on land in what was then known as Pine Creek.

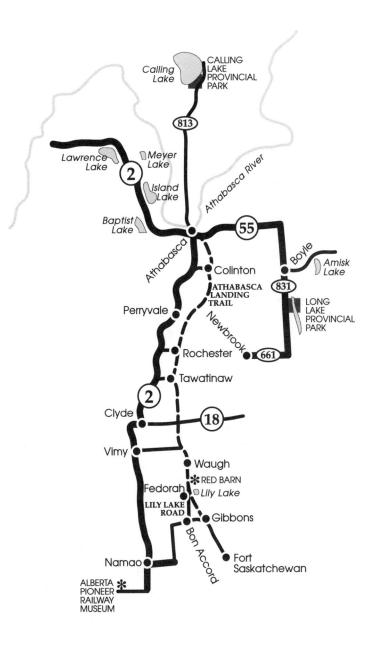

Athabasca Landing Trail

GIBBONS

Rather than driving on a smooth, clean, easily accessible paved highway, why not travel a road that has been used by white people for over 100 years and by Natives for centuries: the

Athabasca Landing Trail Marker

Athabasca Landing Trail from Gibbons to Athabasca. The trail itself started in Edmonton, but most of it has disappeared into farmland between there and Gibbons, so this town is now considered the beginning. While some of the trail cannot be reached by vehicle, you will have an idea of the route by the conclusion of your journey.

Watch for sights, old and new, along the road. The first is the Anglican Church in Gibbons. The unique interior is modelled after the inside of a ship.

Athabasca Landing

The Athabasca Landing Trail intersects the Victoria Trail at Battenburg Crossing on the Sturgeon River, at Kilometre 47 (Mile 28). The original trail angles northwest, so from Gibbons drive towards Bon Accord and turn north on the Lily Lake Road.

BON ACCORD

Two kilometres north of Bon Accord is the Sprout Farms fruit tree nursery. Plum, pear, and apricot trees are raised here, and the owners graft, bud, grow, and sell thirty varieties of apple trees. Among the more conventional bushes sold here are currants, saskatoons, cranberries, and raspberries.

The season begins with planting in the early spring. The farm usually closes around the middle of June, then opens again in the fall. You can pick your own fruit during raspberry season, but since the farm is operated by a busy husband and wife team, it is best if you phone ahead before travelling out there in the summer.

The trail passes through Fedorah at Kilometre 53 (Mile 33). A remnant of the Fedorah post office and store, built in 1914, can still be seen in the hamlet. At Kilometre 55 (Mile 34) is the original Marten homestead.

Camel at Alberta Wildlife Park

The Red Barn and the Alberta Wildlife Park are at Lily Lake. The Red Barn is famous for its Saturday night barbecue and dance. You can really boogie on the 600 square metre (6,400 square foot) maple dance floor, which is surrounded by tables. The second floor consists of tables along the walls and a balcony from which you can watch the band and the dancers on the floor below.

In the same yard is the 68 hectare (168 acre) Wildlife Park with over 2,000 animals and birds from around the world. When you pass through the gates, your eyes will be drawn to the 52 metre (170 foot) tall totem pole projecting from the roof of the log concession. The pillar was hand carved by an Algonquin chief from Ontario and is the tallest totem pole east of Vancouver.

A wide cement path winds between the fenced grounds where camels, giraffes, elk, Siberian tigers, and the other species of animals roam. Plan to spend a day wandering through the park enjoying the birds and animals. If you are there on a Saturday, stay in the campground and attend the dance at the barn.

St. Mary's Romanian Orthodox Church, Waugh

To see one of the best preserved buildings along the trail, drive through Waugh and take the first turn west. Go about 1.6 kilometres (one mile) to the original St. Mary's Church, constructed beside the trail in 1905-07. It is the first Romanian Orthodox Church built in Alberta and the second in North America. It is now a museum. A sign on the fence shows where the Athabasca Landing Trail proceeded north past the church.

Tawatinaw and Rochester

To get onto the trail again, head back to Lily Lake Road, turn north and follow it to the Half Moon Lake store. Turn west. Continue on this road to Vimy on Highway #2 and head to

Tawatinaw; or take the jog north and continue following the trail to Highway #18, turn west to Clyde and then drive to Tawatinaw. The trail ends a short distance north of #18.

Tawatinaw Valley, along Athabasca Landing Trail

At Tawatinaw, head east on the gravel road past the town until you come to an Athabasca Landing Trail sign on a fence post. This is where the trail from the southeast turns north. Travel back southeast for a few kilometres and you will see a farmsite that has been in operation since 1913.

When you arrive at the "T" intersection, turn around and backtrack to where the trail heads north. Along this section, the road is narrow and follows a ridge above Tawatinaw and Rochester, bypassing the present day hamlets. The Athabasca Landing Trail signs are few and far between, so if you begin to wonder whether you are on the right road, stop and ask. The road will eventually take you to Perryvale, Colinton, and Athabasca.

While the Athabasca Landing Trail runs along the top of the valley, it is too far inland for you to enjoy any of the scenery. To see some of the landscape, follow the old gravel highway that passes through the towns. It is about halfway up the valley and, at times, you have a clear view of the creek running below.

Historic Buildings

Many of the historic buildings still survive along the trail: the Zawalykut's homestead at Kilometre 73 (Mile 45); McNelly's homestead, built in 1912 at Kilometre 79 (Mile 49); Gullion School at Kilometre 82 (Mile 51); and Egge's Stopping Place, with a building dating back to 1898, at Kilometre 84 (Mile 52). At Stony Creek Site (Tawatinaw), Kilometre 101 (Mile 63), there are several log buildings. St. Andrew's Anglican Church is in the Kinnoull Park in Colinton. Colinton, Kilometre 147 (Mile 91) was formerly known as Kinnoull. At the end of the trail, Kilometre 160 (Mile 99.5), is the Lessard Stopping Place, constructed in 1912.

Athabasca and District

ATHABASCA

The railway station in Athabasca was erected in 1912 and the brick school house, the United Church, and the Union Hotel

United Church, Athabasca

were all built in 1913. When the United Church was constructed, it was one of the tallest buildings in the West.

Between 1876 and 1903, Athabasca Landing was an important trading centre. It was the connection point between central and northern Alberta and was also the headquarters for northern missionaries of the Anglican Church. During the Klondike gold rush, many people camped at Athabasca Landing on their way over the all-Canadian route to the gold fields.

A park has been created at the original landing site for boats arriving from the north. It has a camp kitchen, picnic and camping areas, and washrooms with hot and cold running water.

Old building along Athabasca Landing Trail

For years, the trail from Edmonton and the Athabasca River were the only means of access to the town. Today, Athabasca is at the cross roads of Highways #2, #55, and #813.

Athabasca Landing Trail

Athabasca Landing was established by the Hudson's Bay Company in 1874. The Company then developed the trail in 1875. It was really a 161 kilometre (100 mile) portage between Fort Edmonton on the North Saskatchewan River and Athabasca Landing on the Athabasca River. • Freight was shipped from Edmonton to Athabasca Landing and sent down the river to points north. Furs were brought back up the waterway to the town, then across the trail to Edmonton. With the coming of the railroad in 1912, the trail fell into disuse. It was revived after the introduction of the automobile.

CALLING LAKE PROVINCIAL PARK

Secondary Highway #813 is paved north to Calling Lake Provincial Park. Soon after leaving Athabasca, you will cross a bridge from which you can see the town nestled on the bank of the river.

Calling Lake Provincial Park

Calling Lake is 20 kilometres (12 miles) long and 18 kilometres (11 miles) wide. The water is pleasant for swimming, boating, and sailing. Perch, whitefish, walleye to 5.5 kilograms (12 pounds) and pike to nine kilograms (20 pounds) make fishing worthwhile.

The park is small but is in a lovely setting, with tall trees, green lawns, and some short hiking trails. There are 28 campsites, and if you walk to the beach and into the trees along the lake, you will find picnic tables with firepits. This is a great place to take photographs of a sunset.

Northwest on Highway #2

Northwest of Athabasca, on Highway #2, is a lake lover's paradise. Twenty kilometres (12 miles) west is Baptiste Lake, with mainly summer villages and private campgrounds for seasonal residents. There are no public campgrounds, but there are day use areas for those who want to visit for an afternoon.

Fishing

Fishing is such a popular sport in Alberta that the demand surpasses the production potential of the lakes, rivers, and streams. The province is ranked eighth in Canada for the quantity of water available for the activity, but is third in the amount of fishing enjoyed each year.

The water is warm, and great for boating and water skiing. Children will love the sandy beach, and there is a burger bar for those who forget their picnic lunches.

Just north of Baptiste Lake, on the east side of the highway, is a Hutterite colony. Round metal granaries, long silver farm buildings, and blue and white community houses make up the settlement. The colony is set in the middle of rolling hills heavy with crops.

Baptiste Lake

The land around Island Lake is also privately owned, but there is a public campground at Ghost Lake, about seven kilometres (4.3 miles) north. For those who want a little more seclusion, travel about 15 kilometres (nine miles) north of Island Lake to Meyer Lake.

Lawrence Lake is very popular. The campground has camping sites, picnic tables, a small recreation area, and boating. Get there early because it usually fills up quickly.

AMBER VALLEY

East of Athabasca, along Highway #55, is Amber Valley, the home of Alberta's first black settlers. Stop for a moment and look out over the wide valley.

In 1910, almost 200 blacks were led into the province by 22-year-old Jefferson Davis Edwards, and they settled on land in what was then known as Pine Creek.

Amber Valley

They had left Oklahoma and discrimination against their race for what they hoped would be a better life. But not everyone welcomed them here. They were advised that the climate was not suitable for them and they should return to the warmer temperatures of the South.

In spite of prejudice, the community increased. A school, a church, and a post office were built. Soon it was the largest black rural community in Alberta and the only one that remained virtually all black.

In 1932, the name was changed to Amber Valley. However, the Depression and the Second World War caused a slow decline in population. Only a few black families remain today. Despite the racial problems he faced, Edwards claimed he never regretted moving to Alberta.

Boyle to Newbrook

BOYLE

Go east of Athabasca to the junction of Highways #55 and #63, then turn south to the town of Boyle. Boyle's main street is made very narrow by the angle parking allowed on both sides. There is a planing mill on the north-west side of town, with a burner and huge piles of lumber stacked in the yard. Lumber from here is shipped around the world.

Outdoor enthusiasts will enjoy the many summer hiking trails in the area and the winter downhill skiing and snowmobiling.

Amisk Lake is 13 kilometres (eight miles) east of Boyle on Highway #663. With a depth of 57 metres (185 feet), it is one of the deepest lakes in northern Alberta. Fishermen might like to try for whitefish and pickerel here.

If you are a student of mycology (mushrooms), the shores of Amisk Lake are an excellent location for viewing fungi. Morels, puffballs, chantarelle, fly amanite, russula, and many other species flourish. Watch the trees for bracket fungi.

LONG LAKE PROVINCIAL PARK

Long Lake Provincial Park is south of Boyle on Highway 831. The park is a lovely place to spend a weekend, or longer. There are 220 camping sites, shady day use areas, a wide, well-kept lawn, and a small confectionery. For the sportsman, there are boat rentals and fishing for northern pike, perch, and walleye.

NEWBROOK

Throughout history, people have been intrigued by stars. Because Alberta's evenings skies are the stage for frequent flashes of shooting stars and meteorites, a meteor observatory was established at Newbrook in 1952. It was equipped with the era's best "fast" cameras, to track the fiery streaks on the long, clear, winter nights. This observatory took North America's first photograph of Sputnik I, the first man-made satellite in orbit.

The station shut down in the early 1970s and its tower was removed. The government sold the land, but the building is still standing. To see it, head south on Highway #831 and west on #661 to Newbrook. Continue west through the town to the railway tracks. Take the first turn south after the tracks.

Newbrook Observatory

The road is only about 100 metres long. It passes an old blue and white house and makes a loop in front of what looks like a long-abandoned chicken coop. That old "chicken coop" is the observatory.

The station was constructed on two levels. In the higher room, the cement pedestal where the cameras where attached sits in the middle of the floor. The scientists reached the cameras by climbing three small steps formed in the cement. Rusted pulleys and wires, once used to open the roof, hang in the corners of the room. The roof didn't slide sideways or fold upwards — it was peaked in the centre and slid down runners towards the ground.

Chapter 9
Lac La Biche to Fort Chipewyan

The boreal forest in this segment of Alberta is laden with lakes. There are over a dozen bodies of water within driving distance of Lac La Biche. Fly-in sportfishing is very popular in the Fort McMurray region because of the seven trophy lakes close by.

Many birds dwell in Sir Winston Churchill Provincial Park, including goshawks, ruby-throated hummingbirds, broad-winged hawks, and winter wrens. For a pleasant afternoon, relax on a bench overlooking the lake and watch the various birds glide by.

Just north of Wandering River is a sign reading: "Game Farm, No Trespassing, No Hunting, No Shooting for the next 2 kilometres." A tall wire fence has been erected on a hill about a quarter of a kilometre back from the road. If you are lucky, you will be able to se elk grazing behind it.

Gregoire Lake Provincial Park is on a deep-blue coloured lake, and has a long beach, a boat launch, hiking trails, and an observation deck overlooking the water. For the angler, there are walleye, perch, whitefish, and pike.

Thern are six fly-in fishing lodges within 50 kilometres (90 miles) of Fort McMurray, three of which are based in the city. Some of the lodges are also open in the winter. Christina Lake, one of the trophy lakes, can be reached by a gravel road south of the town.

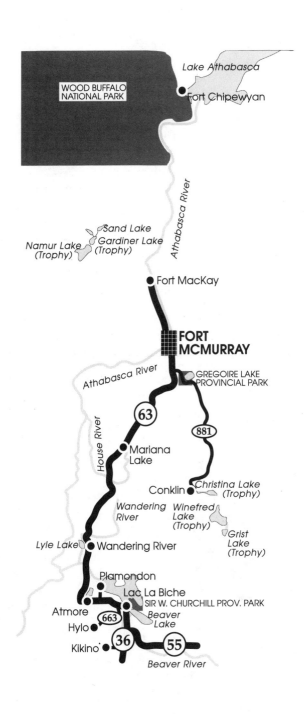

Lac La Biche and District

LAC LA BICHE

Red Deer's Lake House was established by the North West Company on Lac La Biche, in 1798. The Hudson's Bay Company built Greenwich House in 1799, but by 1800, both were abandoned. A permanent post was eventually constructed in 1853 by the Hudson's Bay Company.

Lac La Biche has a long and varied history, but one of the historic sites you won't be able to visit is the Lac La Biche Inn, which burned down in 1988. A replica, with some changes, has since been constructed on Churchill Drive and 100th Street, overlooking the lake. Its colour is the same as the original, yellow with a green roof, but it now houses the town offices, a library and archives, meeting rooms, and a tourist information centre.

Lac La Biche Inn

The hotel opened in 1916, but closed again in 1918, due to problems with rooms and a boating accident which caused considerable controversy. Nineteen years later, it reopened as a hospital and was subsequently converted into a nurse's residence. In 1985 restoration began on the structure, which had been acquired by the town. The repairs had almost been completed when a fire destroyed the building on April 21, 1988.

Alberta has the third largest Arab population in Canada and many live in Lac La Biche. They have erected one of the few Muslim mosques in Alberta on Highway #36 south.

Sir Winston Churchill Provincial Park

Sir Winston Churchill Provincial Park is on an island 8.5 kilometres (5 miles) northeast of the town, and is linked to land by a 2.5 kilometre (1.5 mile), man-made causeway. A long, winding drive through tall trees will get you to the picnic areas, beaches, camping sites, and Pelican Point. Through a telescope, you can view the tiny island populated with pelicans and cormorants.

Hiking trails will guide you through an eastern boreal forest, not commonly seen in Alberta. The principal tree is the balsam fir, with white spruce, paper birch, and aspen making up the remaining timberland.

Many birds dwell in the park, including goshawks, ruby-throated hummingbirds, broad-winged hawks, and winter wrens. For a pleasant afternoon, relax on a bench overlooking the lake and watch the various birds glide by.

The narrow strip of land between Lac La Biche and Beaver Lake, just south of the town of Lac La Biche, separates the Hudson's Bay and Arctic Ocean drainage systems. The Beaver River drains Beaver Lake and flows east to the Churchill River and Hudson's Bay.

La Biche River issues from Lac La Biche into the Athabasca River, which proceeds north to Lake Athabasca. The combined waters leave the lake through the Slave River and run into the MacKenzie River, finally spilling into the Arctic Ocean.

Both Lac La Biche and Beaver Lake have northern pike, walleye, and perch in their waters.

KIKINO MÉTIS SETTLEMENT

Thirty-nine kilometres (24 miles) south of Lac La Biche on Highway #36 is the Kikino Métis settlement. The settlers have developed a bison, elk, and deer game ranch on their land. Stop at the band office for directions to the paddocks and you will either be given instructions or taken on a guided tour.

HYLO AND LAC LA BICHE MISSION

Hylo is southwest of Lac La Biche on Highway #663. The hamlet received its name when the railway was being constructed. The crews took pleasure in a friendly hand of poker after the day's work and their favourite game was High-Low.

Hylo Museum

Drop in at the hardware and grocery store for coffee. Cake donuts and slices of garlic sausage are set on a table for customers to sample while shopping.

West of the store is a museum with a large steam engine sitting in front. The engine was brought from the United States by its owner, but it can't be operated on the streets or highways because of its cleated steel tires.

About 11 kilometres (6.5 miles) west of Lac La Biche is the Lac La Biche mission. In 1853, Father Remas of the Oblate Missionaries established Notre Dame des Victoires in a small cabin beside the Hudson's Bay Company's post. The mission was moved in 1855 to its present site and became the home base for priests with missions in the Mackenzie River, Peace, and Athabasca regions.

The parish settlement expanded to include a flour mill, a printing press, farmland, a boat construction area, a saw mill, warehouses, and a school and convent operated by the Sisters of Charity (Grey Nuns). By the end of the century,

Lac La Biche Misson

though, this religious headquarters had lost its prominence in the north and soon faded into the background of history.

The mission is on a slight hill overlooking the lake. Services are still held in the well-preserved church on Sundays and the remaining buildings have been restored.

Walk across the road to the cemetery. A fence encloses the graves, but the gate is not locked. Some of the headstones are so time-worn, the lettering on them has faded. The oldest graves that can be read are of a baby who died in 1885 and a three-year-old boy who died in 1892.

Reverend Henry Bird Steinhauer

Lac La Biche was the initial western posting of Reverend Henry Bird Steinhauer, the first Ojibway to be ordained as a minister. He hoped to teach his people to farm, but found the land around Lac La Biche to be mostly swampy bush. To realize his dream, he moved to Whitefish Lake and started the earliest permanent Native settlement in Alberta. He was the grandfather of Ralph Steinhauer, the first Native person to become Lieutenant-Governor of the Province of Alberta.

Plamondon to Marianna Lake

PLAMONDON AND ATMORE

The Plamondon Museum is located in a tiny, original church in town. Watch on the south side of the highway for the Atmore Shrine, just before Atmore. Tall trees stand along one side and a lovely lawn spreads out in front.

The first few kilometres of Highway #63 to Fort McMurray follow the shore of Charron Lake. You will travel by new farm houses and old buildings left by past residents, and pass through fields and over rivers.

After Wandering River, the number of farms decreases. Except for two burn areas, tall, green trees or thick bush line the highway most of the way to Fort McMurray. You will not be alone on this road — traffic is moderate and everyone seems to travel at a high speed.

There are roadside turnouts about every 15 kilometres (nine miles). There are also several camping sites and recreation areas at which you can stop and rest. A person might get bored on the drive to Fort McMurray, but there is no reason to be tired.

Atmore Shrine

If you stop at a roadside turn out to relax, gently close your door. The atmosphere is so still that any sound will vibrate off the wall of trees on each side of the road. Inhale deeply and enjoy the smell of the evergreens and the fresh clean air. After a few minutes, birds will begin singing and soon the forest will be full of their different songs and calls.

WANDERING RIVER AND MARIANNA LAKE

At the hamlet of Wandering River, Judy's Country Classic Restaurant is open 24 hours a day. The BigWay Foods store has a bakery where pizza is prepared, cooked, and sold. There is also a large selection of baked goods.

Just north of Wandering River is a sign reading: "Game Farm, No Trespassing, No Hunting, No Shooting for the next 2 kilometres." A tall wire fence has been erected on a hill about a quarter of a kilometre back from the road. If you are lucky, you will be able to see elk grazing behind it.

A large burn area begins at kilometre 62 (mile 38). It continues for over 10 kilometres (six miles) along the highway. Although the land is covered by tall, blackened derelict trees with gray, bare, branches, you will notice small, new trees sprouting alongside the deadwood.

There is a recreation area beside House River and another just south of Marianna Lake. Marianna Lake has a service station, a grocery store, a cafe, and a lounge. North of the hamlet is another burn area.

Fort McMurray and District

GREGOIRE LAKE PROVINCIAL PARK

Gregoire Lake Provincial Park is 40 kilometres (24 miles) south of Fort McMurray. The park is on a deep-blue coloured lake, and has a long beach, a boat launch, hiking trails, and an observation deck overlooking the waters. For the angler, there are walleye, perch, whitefish, and pike.

Plant life ranges from bogs in the northwest to tall spruce and fir trees. There is a magnificent stand of paper birch on the northeast side. The rare round-leaved bog orchid *Habenaria orbiculata* can be found in this grove.

Gregoire Lake Provincial Park

Although big game and waterfowl hunting is poor in the Fort McMurray area, hunters and gun enthusiasts keep in practice at the gun range 17 kilometres (10.5 miles) north of the park. About 12 kilometres (7.5 miles) further is the turn off to the modern airport and downhill ski slopes.

FORT MCMURRAY

Fort McMurray was established in 1870 by Henry John Moberly, a Hudson's Bay Company employee. He was sent south by the factor of Fort Chipewyan to open a post at the forks of the Athabasca and Clearwater Rivers. Moberly built the fort, which burned down in 1872 and had to be reconstructed. While there, Moberly found a salt bed about 24 kilometres (15 miles) from the post.

The first sternwheeler to run the Athabasca river from Fort McMurray to Fort Chipewyan was the *Grahame*. It was constructed in Fort Chipewyan in 1883. Steamboats kept the town alive until the railroad reached

Fort McMurray Interpretive Centre

a point 12.8 kilometres (8 miles) to the south, in 1922. Salt extraction and fishing were the two main industries, until the oil project began.

At the Fort McMurray Interpretive Centre, opened in 1985, you will see a multi-media presentation on the history of the industry and the procedures used to extract the oil. Two computer games reproduce the process, and there are models, photographs, and artifacts to see.

Oil Sands

The Athabasca Oil Sands cover an area of 29,260 square kilometres (11,254 square miles) at an average depth of 600 metres (1,950 feet). It is estimated that they contain 700 billion barrels of oil. Surface mining, the only method used so far, will only work about 1/10th of the area because it only works on sand not more than 60 metres (195 feet) deep. • The Natives and early settlers used tar from the oil sands to repair their boats, but it was not until the 1870s that the sands were first explored. And it wasn't until a hot water oil separation process was developed in the 1920s that they were seriously worked. • For many years, different means of removing the oil from the sands were tried. Some were successful, others were not. In 1941, Abasand Oils produced 21,476 barrels of oil with a maximum rate of 200 barrels a day. It was closed in 1945, when a fire raged through the plant. • In 1947, two plant sites were built by the government at Bitumount, 89 kilometres (55 miles) from Fort McMurray. Although the town of Fort McMurray did not boom until the 1970s, these ventures were the predecessors of the Fort McMurray Oil Sands project.

Go to the J. Howard Pew Industrial Garden to view some of the huge machinery employed to wrest the oil from the sand. Take one of the tours by four-wheel drive out to Bitumont, the initial extraction site. There you will see some of the earliest equipment used and the old plant.

After viewing Bitumont, try a bus tour of the Suncor and the Syncrude Canada sites to compare the old and the new. These excursions can be arranged at the visitors' bureau.

Drop in to Heritage Park, where displays depict Fort McMurray in its early days when trapping, fishing, logging, and salt mining were the main sources of income. There are a dozen buildings to visit, hundreds of photographs to view, and riverboats to examine.

Heritage Park, Fort McMurray

Drive to the docks, where barges still carry supplies to Fort Chipewyan on the Athabasca River, or take part in one of the many activities held throughout the summer. Heritage Day includes children's games, multicultural food to sample, and a costume contest. The Blueberry Festival in September starts with a pancake breakfast, and carries on with a midway, country fair, soapbox derby, fireworks, and the crowning of Miss Blueberry.

There are six fly-in fishing lodges within 150 kilometres (90 miles) of Fort McMurray, three of which are based in the city. Some of the lodges are also open in the winter. Christina Lake, one of the trophy lakes, can be reached by a gravel road south of the town.

Fifty kilometres (30 miles) north of the city is the Oil Sands Viewpoint. Watch for it on the east side of the road and be prepared for a bumpy drive as it is a steep, gravel, predominantly washboard, hill. The lookout is enclosed by a metal fence, and two telescopes allow you to view the excavation area. You can see the machines working far below in the deep pits.

Across the road is the Syncrude plant, with its tall smoke stacks and huge cranes. About a kilometre past the viewpoint is the driveway into the plant. Here the pavement ends and you continue on gravel.

FORT MCKAY

Descend into the McKay River valley and cross a bridge to reach the hamlet of Fort McKay. Beware of the large holes and bumps on the main street.

Archaeologists have found evidence in the Beaver River quarry near Fort Mckay that the area was occupied by people as far back as 8,000 to 10,000 years ago.

Fort Chipewyan and District

FORT CHIPEWYAN

The only way to reach Fort Chipewyan in the summer is by airplane. There are two ways to reach it in winter—by airplane or by driving on a winter road over frozen muskeg and river delta. There is a daily flight by Time Air from Fort McMurray to Fort Chipewyan.

The view from the plane to Fort Chipewyan is excellent. Rivers snake through the mass of trees and two large sand dunes are a bright yellow against the green. As you near Fort Chipewyan, you can see the deep blue of Lake Athabasca. The plane lands at a small airport outside town and the town's only taxi is waiting for anyone who wants a ride.

Fort Chipewyan has a population of over 900 people. It is a modern town with the honour of being set on the only location in Alberta where the rock of the pre-Cambrian Shield protrudes above the earth's crust. There is a new lodge, built on the pre-Cambrian Shield overlooking the lake, and two motels for tourists. You have to book ahead as they are very popular.

A cairn to fur traders is framed against the sky on top of Monument Hill, which rises above the immense Lake Athabasca.

Peter Pond

In 1778, a group of independent fur traders decided to send an American fur trader, Peter Pond, into the Athabasca region. This was an area known only from tales told by the natives. Pond left Cumberland House, west of Lake Winnipeg, and followed a route of many twisting streams and about 80 portages. The worst was the 20 kilometre (12 mile) Methye Portage, which separates the Arctic and Hudson's Bay watersheds. On the other side of the portage was the Clearwater River. • Pond and his companions travelled west on the dangerous Clearwater River until they reached the smoother waters of the Athabasca. They stopped about 48 kilometres (30 miles) south of Lake Athabasca, constructed the first known European's house in Alberta and stayed for the winter. While there, Pond traded for furs with the Natives and, by spring, had more than he could safely transport East. He cached some until his return in the fall. • Pond was the initial explorer of the Athabasca Oil Sands area. His early maps showed tar deposits in the region that would later become famous for its oil sands.

Fort Chipewyan is the oldest European settlement in Alberta. It was established in 1788 and owes its origin to the fur trade.

In 1784, independent traders formed the North West Company, which took over the post on the Athabasca River. In 1788, the first Fort Chipewyan was established on the shore of Lake Athabasca. It was named after the natives who resided in the area.

Fort Chipewyan Lodge

Trapping and trading were completed during the winter and brigades of canoes laden with furs left the fort in the spring to make the long voyage to Grand Portage on the western tip of Lake Superior.

Besides being a fur trading post, Fort Chipewyan was also the jumping off point for Alexander Mackenzie in his attempts to find an overland route to the Pacific Ocean.

In 1799, the fort was moved to the north side of Lake Athabasca, the site of present-day Fort Chipewyan. When the Hudson's Bay Company and the North West Company amalgamated in 1821, many forts were closed, but Fort Chipewyan survived. It became the Hudson's Bay Company's command post for the Athabasca and Mackenzie River basins.

Chapter 10
Redwater to Cold Lake

Many lakes near this highway contain northern pike, walleye, pickerel, perch, whitefish, and trout in their waters. Don't attempt angling in such lakes as Lottie, north of Ashmont; Smoky, west of Smoky Lake; and Marguerite, north of Cold Lake — they will prove to be unproductive. The land on both sides of the highway is good for deer, moose, ruffled and spruce grouse, goose, and duck hunting.

South and east of Redwater is a section of the Victoria Trail, which ran from Edmonton to Victoria Settlement during the 1800s. It is an enjoyable drive along the trail where Natives once walked and where the settlers travelled in Red River carts.

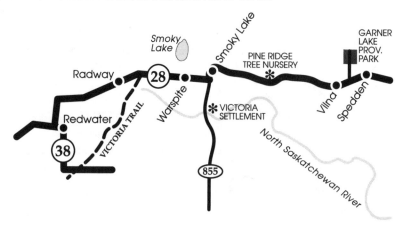

North of Vilna and Spedden are a number of excellent fishing, boating, and swimming lakes. Most have camping facilities. The 9-hole Vilna golf course is near the Bonnie Lake Provincial Campsite. The Garner Lake Provincial Park has 66 sites and is open all year for day use.

The Therien Lakes, just south of St. Paul, are a bird watcher's dream. A ring billed and California gull colony resides on Upper Therien Lake and two double crested cormorant colonies are located on Lower Therien. At nearby Lac Canard is a concentration of cormorants, great blue herons, and grackles. Also, a large flock of non-breeding white pelicans use the area as a feeding ground during the summer. A few of the rarer birds found here are turkey vultures, American bitterns, western grebes, and black-crowned herons.

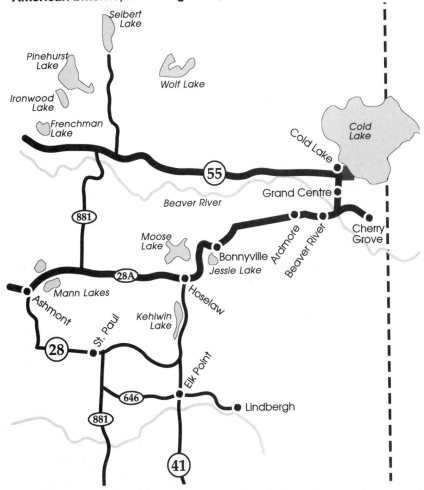

Redwater to Ashmont

Redwater is situated in one of Alberta's major oilfields, and oil pumps stroke throughout the town. D-Days, a salute to the oil industry, is celebrated in August with a pancake breakfast, golf tournament, rodeo, dance, and many more activities. The town has erected what it claims to be the tallest oil derrick in North America. It is on 53rd Street and 48th Avenue.

South and east of Redwater is a section of the Victoria Trail, which ran from Edmonton to Victoria Settlement during the 1800s. *Oil pump*

To reach the trail, go east through Redwater and turn south on Highway #38. Follow it to Township Road #570. Head east, and about three kilometres (1.8 miles) down the road is a Victoria Trail sign pointing south. If you want to drive the pathway from the start, follow the gravel road the few kilometres to its beginning at Range Road #214.

It is an enjoyable drive along the trail where Natives once walked and where the settlers travelled in Red River carts. They would probably be very surprised at the changes in some of the scenery: the large, modern homes, the big barns, the rows of metal granaries, the machine sheds with their full line of farming machinery, the open fields of grain, and the animals. The biting smell from the barn yards would certainly be unlike the sweet smell of flowers, trees, and open air to which they were accustomed.

Old building on Victoria Trail

When you arrive back at Township Road #570, turn east and watch for the Victoria Trail sign on the north side. Shortly after turning onto the gravel road, you will cross a one lane green bridge. The few farms located at the beginning of the trail are soon replaced by trees and open spaces. Old log dwellings, that might date back to the time of the early homesteaders, lean at precarious angles in some of the meadows.

Victoria Trail is about 11 kilometres (seven miles) long and ends at Range Road #203. You can turn back to Highway #38, or follow #203 until you come to a sign saying "No Exit." Turn west and continue to the first turn north. From there, it is a few kilometres to Highway #28, by Radway.

Red River Carts

Red River carts were made entirely of wood and tied together with leather. The two wheels were about 1.5 metres (five feet) in diameter and the box, slung on the axle, could carry 363 kilograms (800 pounds). The axles could not be greased because dust and dirt would collect in them and prevent the wheels from turning. Consequently, they squealed continuously. • The carts were pulled by horse or ox and were used by the early settlers to carry supplies overland. The carts' basic construction made them easy to dismantle and float across rivers.

Smoky Lake

The town of Smoky Lake was named for the nearby lake which was initially called Smoking Lake by the Cree. There are two accounts of how the lake received its name. In one version, Natives who stopped by its shores and smoked their pipes during their hunts, called it Smoking Place. In the other, it was selected because the mist lifting off the lake resembled rising smoke.

Smoky Lake once made it into Ripley's *Believe It or Not*. For a short period in its history, the town had the greatest number of businesses per capita in Canada.

Historic Victoria Settlement, at the end of the Victoria Trail, is south of Smoky Lake on Highway #855. After a few kilometres you will come to a campsite on the east side of the highway, dedicated to the homesteaders and settlers of the Victoria Settlement school district. On a monument at the entrance are the names of the first teachers, the years they taught, and the names of the students.

The school district was organized in 1888, and in 1919, the school was moved from its original site to this one. To preserve their heritage, the members of the Victoria Community Centre bought this land in 1960 and turned it into a picnic ground. The school was relocated to Smoky Lake and now contains a museum.

Continue down Highway #855 to the turn to Victoria Settlement. Your drive from the highway to this famous colony is on another section of the original Victoria Trail.

Victoria Settlement

Reverend Thomas Woolsey, a Methodist missionary, founded a mission at Smoky Lake in 1861. In 1862, he and Rev. George McDougall moved the mission to the North Saskatchewan

Clerk's Quarters, Victoria Settlement

River, 19 kilometres (12 miles) to the south, and called it Victoria in honour of the Queen.

The Hudson's Bay company established a fort near the religious colony in 1864. It ceased operation in 1883, but reopened in 1887, only to close permanently in 1897.

When a post office was opened in 1887, the name Victoria was confused with Victoria, B.C. The community was re-named Pakan in honour of a Cree chief who had refused to join in the 1885 North West (Riel) Rebellion.

Victoria/Pakan thrived, but the railroad bypassed it in 1918 and slowly businesses moved north to the rail line. A new town called Smoky Lake was founded near Woolsey's first mission.

The white building in the trees is the clerk's quarters, built by the Hudson's Bay Company in 1864. It is Alberta's oldest structure still on its original foundation. The quarters have been restored and on the inside walls you can see where Hudson's Bay employees carved their initials.

Also at the settlement are the graves of Rev. George McDougall's three daughters and his daughter-in-law, who died in the 1870 small-pox epidemic. The small Pakan Church, constructed in 1906, is now used as an interpretive centre at the site.

Smallpox

The Natives of the North had no defense against the settlers' diseases. When the plagues were carried across the countryside, they destroyed entire bands. One smallpox epidemic occurred in 1837, when the sickness travelled up the Missouri on the *St. Peter*, an American Fur Company's steamboat. It was transferred to other boats and then to Natives who had come to trade. They, in turn, carried the virus north to their people. • In one Peigan camp, sixty lodges were wiped out and only two women survived. The death rate of Bloods and Blackfoot, camped where Lethbridge is today, was so high they named the grounds the Grave Yard. By the time the disease had swept north, 6,000 of the 9,000 members of the Blackfoot Confederacy were dead. • The dreaded killer struck again in 1869, and by 1870, had crossed the plains. When the Natives, in their fear, gathered at Victoria Mission, Reverend John McDougall tried to convince them to stay away from each other, so they wouldn't spread the disease. Although this helped save some lives, by the end of the epidemic, half of Alberta's Native people, as well as many whites and Métis, were dead.

Stroll along the asphalt paths, under the spreading branches of the tall maples planted during the early years of the post. Bring a lunch and have a picnic on the large lawn. Or grab your fishing gear and hike down the wide path to the North Saskatchewan River. You can stand and fish from the banks where the fur traders beached their canoes over 100 years ago.

Twenty kilometres (12 miles) east of Smoky Lake, on Highway #28, is the Pine Ridge Forest Nursery. This nursery is the largest of its type in North America and is regarded as the leader in technological growth in its field. Situated on 113 hectares (280 acres), it has 20 greenhouses that raise white spruce and lodgepole pine for reforestation throughout Alberta. During the summer, tours are available from Monday to Friday between 8:30 and 4:30. The young trees, though, are not for private sale.

VILNA, SPEDDEN, AND ASHMONT

North of Vilna and Spedden are a number of excellent fishing, boating, and swimming lakes. Most have camping facilities. The 9-hole Vilna golf course is near the Bonnie Lake Provincial Campsite. The Garner Lake Provincial Park has 66 sites and is open all year for day use.

Ashmont hosts an annual "Buck of the Year" contest, the largest of its type in Alberta. It was founded in 1979 and the original competition was conducted on a bench outside the Ashmont Sport and Gift Shop. Now, the participants assemble at the Legion Hall for the judging, followed by a dinner and dance.

As many as 200 heads are divided into two categories: typical and non-typical. In the typical class, the horns are closely balanced, while mismatched antlers are assigned to the non-typical division. Prizes are awarded to the winners in the muley and whitetail typical and non-typical sections. Hunters come from across northern Alberta to enter and try for a Boone and Crockett record. (Boone and Crockett entrants are scored by an official who measures the length and circumference of the horns and counts the number of tines).

Highway #28A

MANN LAKES AND SEIBERT LAKE

At Ashmont the highway number changes to 28A as far as Hoselaw. It crosses two railway tracks and winds through the Upper and Lower Mann Lakes. No matter what the season, you will almost always find someone fishing the upper lake for pike, walleye, or perch. The fish in Lower Mann on the north side of the road have a tendency to die off in winter and the catch is usually poor.

The birch trees on the island in Upper Mann Lake are a popular nesting site for birds. Besides the more common fowl, great crested fly catchers have been seen on the island.

If you want to try your luck for northern pike, whitefish, pickerel, walleye, and perch on a trophy lake, turn off #28A at #881. Follow it to #55 and head east. Watch for the Seibert Lake sign, pointing north.

The first section of road is fairly good gravel. But when you turn onto the sand surfaced forestry road, watch our for deep holes, usually filled with water. Do not attempt this journey with a car unless the weather has been extremely dry. You will find a lovely lake and a good campsite at the end of your drive, if you make it.

GLENDON

Eight kilometres (five miles) north of #28A is the village of Glendon, now known as the "Perogy Capital of Alberta." Standing in Perogy Park, on Perogy Drive, is the world's largest

perogy. It was unveiled on August 31, 1991 to coincide with the beginning of the nation-wide celebrations commemorating the 100th anniversary of Ukrainian settlement in Canada.

The perogy, made of steel and fibreglass, was constructed in Salmon Arm, B.C. and cost an estimated $60,000. Many of the businesses in the village have been renamed to include the word perogy and if you want a sample of Ukrainian fare, visit the Perogy House across from the park.

World's largest perogy, Glendon

St. Paul to Hoselaw

ST. PAUL

Highway #28 continues from Ashmont to the St. Bride corner then swings east to St. Paul. While in St. Paul, watch for unidentified flying objects hovering aloft, waiting for an opportunity to land on the world's first and only man-made UFO landing pad.

UFO landing pad, St. Paul.

The 12 metre (39 foot), circular platform, with provincial and territorial flags flying overhead, stands expectantly on the corner of 50th Avenue (Highway #28) and 53rd Street. It was erected as a centennial project in 1967, and a time capsule inside the pad is to be opened in 2067.

The St. Paul Cultural Centre is Alberta's first bilingual cultural centre. It has a museum, an art gallery with displays by local artists, and is the home of a folklore dance group, "Les Blés d'Or."

Raising Money

On a street near Jean Louis Lagasse Park is a two-storey, Spanish style house erected by the diocese of St. Paul and other organizations and sold to a private family. Through this and additional projects, over a million dollars has been raised for Mother Theresa's work in the third world. Four of Mother Theresa's nuns from the Missionaries of Charity reside in the town.

The Therien Lakes, just south of St. Paul, are a bird watcher's dream. A ring billed and California gull colony resides on Upper Therien Lake and two double crested cormorant colonies are located on Lower Therien. At nearby Lac Canard is a concentration of cormorants, great blue herons, and grackles. Also, a large flock of non-breeding white pelicans use the area as a feeding grounds during the summer. A few of the rarer birds found here are turkey vultures, American bitterns, western grebes, and black-crowned herons.

Alas, for the fisherman, there are no fish in the Therien Lakes.

Would you like to sample some sparkling spring water right out of the ground? Take Highway #881 south of St. Paul to the North Saskatchewan River. Cross the bridge and drive almost to the crest of the hill. Watch on the west side for a turnout with a white fence, garbage barrels, and the sign "Myrnam Spring."

The Old Rectory, St. Paul

A sloping sidewalk leads down to the clear water, flowing like a mountain stream from a culvert. Satisfy your thirst with the cool, fresh liquid and fill some plastic jugs for future use.

Head back north to #646, a gravel road that cuts across country to Highway #41. You will end up just south of Elk Point. West of present-day Elk Point is the site of the first fur trading posts built along the North Saskatchewan River in Alberta.

To visit the sites, continue east along #646 for about eight kilometres (five miles) or until you come to the gravel pile on the south side of the highway. Turn south, then take the first road east. Carry on past A's Driving Range and turn south again onto the gravel road. Follow it to the interpretive centre.

Mural, Elk Point

Inside the centre is a life-size, partial replica of the fort, a canoe, a teepee, and a trading room. Self-guided paths lead from the centre to the sites of both Fort George and Buckingham House.

Fort George was constructed by the North West Company in 1792. The Hudson's Bay Company post, Buckingham House, was built just 54 metres (175 feet) west later that same year. Both forts were situated on a plateau overlooking the North Saskatchewan River and the fur traders had the difficult task of hauling their supplies up the hill from their canoes. The posts did, however, have a beautiful view of the river valley.

In spite of the rivalry between the companies, the forts shared a common well and the traders helped each other in times of hardship.

Archaeological Dig

Fort George and Buckingham House have been popular archaeological sites for years. During past summers, it was not unusual to come upon university students bent over rectangular, metal trays sifting through the soil from their digs. Many of their finds were beads, but thousands of other artifacts, including a few tools, were discovered.

Nine kilometres (5.5 miles) further east on Highway #646 is Lindbergh. The Windsor Salt Plant has the words "Salt of the Earth" painted on its roof. The plant has been in operation since 1948 and produces almost 400 tons of salt every day. The salt bed is about 830 metres (2,700 feet) underground and is over 300 metres (975 feet) thick. It is estimated that there is enough salt in this area to keep Canada supplied for 2,000 years.

Back on Highway #41, head north into Elk Point. Watch for the nine metre (30 foot) tall statue of Peter Fidler, one of the early explorers in the area, at the entrance to the town. The small white building across from the tourist information booth houses the Fort George Museum.

In the park on 50th Avenue and 52nd Street, you will find 10 murals in a curve covering a distance of 30 metres (100 feet). The combined picture, painted by Billie Milholland, tells the history of Elk Point from the voyageurs to present day.

Highway #41 joins with Highway #28 from St. Paul about nine kilometres (5.5 miles) north of Elk Point.

There are two campsites on Kehewin Lake. At the south end of the lake a road leads to the Elk Point Elks Wilderness Park. The park was opened in 1980 and has a boat launch, dock, picnic tables, camping sites, and a fish cleaning table. A public campsite is further north along #41. Stop and try for the perch, northern pike, and walleye in the lake.

As you drive towards Hoselaw, watch for the house on the west side with the teepee fence. Miniature white replicas of Native houses are nailed to the rails of the brown log fence. Each one has a buffalo painted on it in either red, blue, green, or yellow and has matching coloured sticks at the top to represent the poles. The fence encloses a large yard and there are nearly 100 teepees on it.

Bonnyville to Cold Lake

BONNYVILLE

The old Duclos Hospital and a nurse's residence is south of Highway #28, just before the town of Bonnyville. When several French families decided to convert to Protestantism in 1916, they asked Rev. John Duclos to be their pastor. The Duclos Mission was his base as he served this community and many others in the Bonnyville/Cold Lake/St. Paul area. For twenty-five years, he built schools, churches, and hospitals. The Duclos Hospital remained in use until the new Bonnyville Health Centre was opened in 1986.

North Shore Drive in Bonnyville follows the shore of Jessie Lake. Camp beside the lake and let your children have a contest to see who can catch the most fish from a separate, stocked pond.

Take a stroll on the sidewalk along the shore and listen to the songs and chatter of the many birds on the water. Diving and dabbling ducks, yellow-headed and red-winged blackbirds, soras, willets, avocets, and dowitchers are just a few of the birds you will see. Several groups of birds use the lake as a stop-over on their flight north. The red-necked phalarope, a rare species, rests at the lake on its migration from the Gulf of Mexico to the Arctic.

Bonnyville sponsors the Tradex, the largest rural trade fair in Alberta, in June. Hundreds of displays are featured in the Agriplex and a midway will fulfill your desire for excitement. Evening dances are held and a Miss Tradex is crowned.

Northwest of Bonnyville is Moose Lake Provincial Park. Set in the midst of tall jackpine, the park has sandy soil, great beaches, and blue waters.

Shaw House

On the shores of Moose Lake are the remains of Shaw House. In 1789, Angus Shaw established a trading post, called Lac d'Original, for the North West Company on a long point on the north shore of Moose Lake. It was one of the first forts in Alberta, and Shaw ran it for three years. Some people claim the first house built in Alberta was at this post. • All that you would see, should you decide to look for Shaw House, is a pile of rocks that were once the fireplace and a depression from the cellar.

BEAVER RIVER

Eight kilometres (five miles) east of Ardmore is a sign for the Cold Lake First Nations Reserve on the south side of the highway. About seven kilometres (four miles) further are the signs "Beaverdam," with an arrow pointing south and "Beaver River" pointing north.

At one time, Beaver River was known as Le Goff, but the Natives of the reserve felt the community was not entitled to use that name. Periodically, someone (no one knows who) would remove the "Le Goff" highway markers. When replaced by the Department of Highways, the signs inevitably disappeared again. The new signs for "Beaver River" have not been touched.

Right to a Name

During the North West (Riel) Rebellion of 1885, Wandering Spirit, a War Chief under Big Bear, Chief of the Cree, led his band in the killing of nine men at Frog Lake. They looted and burned the buildings and captured prisoners. Joined by their cousins, the Wood Cree and the Chipewyans from Cold Lake, they headed for Fort Pitt. They looted the post, then started north. • After some skirmishes with the Alberta Field Force under General Thomas Bland Strange, the bands split up, with the Cold Lake Chipewyans returning to their reserve. General Strange and the Alberta Field Force trooped to Cold Lake to arrest the tribe. Several members surrendered under their priest, Father LeGoff.

Continue along Highway #28 until you come to a curving hill, called the Beaver River Hill, which descends into the Beaver River Valley. The Beaver River was one of the river routes canoed by the voyageurs during the fur trade era.

Residents of the area still paddle the river today, starting at the bridges north of Bonnyville or Ardmore. If you decide to try it, count on spending a full day if you leave from the Ardmore bridge or two days if you leave from the Bonnyville bridge. The river has a considerable number of bends and twists and the trip takes longer than most people expect.

Eight kilometres (five miles) east of the junction of Highways #28 and #55 is Cherry Grove, and the Grove Greenhouse with its wide variety of flowers and plants. The greenhouse is open for the months of May and June.

GRAND CENTRE

Grand Centre is the main shopping centre for the residents of C.F.B. Cold Lake. On the town's 25th anniversary, the base donated a CF-104 Starfighter to Grand Centre, in recognition of all the years of co-existence between the two communities. The plane "prepares for takeoff" at the lights on the highway.

CF-104 Starfighter, Grand Centre

The golf course is two kilometres (1.2 miles) east of the town and a ski hill, complete with chalet and lifts, is 10 kilometres (six miles) east.

For those who aren't satisfied with the fishing in area lakes, there is fly-in fishing at Winnifred Lake, a trophy lake north of town.

When you leave Grand Centre heading north, watch for the sun glinting off the cross prepared for Pope John Paul's visit to Edmonton in 1984. After the event, the Knights of Columbus in Cold Lake bought the religious symbol and erected it in the field of one of their members.

Just past the cross is one of the few rural drive-ins remaining in the province. It shows double features on Friday, Saturday, and Sunday nights.

COLD LAKE

As you travel the last two kilometres of Highway #28, you will be driving through the town of Cold Lake. The pavement ends at the shore of Cold Lake and near a pair of tall, painted totem poles. Behind the totem poles is the Cold Lake Marina, where 300 boats can be secured in safe moorings. At the store, you can rent boats and purchase fishing licenses, fishing supplies, live bait, and marine supplies.

Stroll down the wide boardwalk to the beginning of the Kinosoo Trail. Follow the man-made path along the rocky shore of the lake and you will end up at the Kinosoo Beach and Playground, where the sand seems endless and the water is refreshingly cool.

The tourist information booth and Grandma's Country Crafts are in an A-frame building on the hill beside the marina. Before entering, stand on the deck for a sweeping view of the marina, with brightly coloured boats and clear, blue, water stretching into the horizon. Inside, every available space is taken up with crafts ranging from painting to crocheting and ceramics to weaving.

The lake is approximately 24 kilometres (15 miles) wide, 32 kilometres (20 miles) long, and can reach depths of 90 metres (300 feet). Because of its size, it is a "cold" lake. Sailing, wind surfing, boating, and canoeing are popular sports on the water, but only the hardy try swimming.

The town of Cold Lake stages an Aqua Days celebration on the long weekend in August. There are many events and races to watch, but the funniest is the non-boat race. Entrants must have a craft that will float and can be manoeuvred through the water without a motor. The

Totem pole

size can vary from one person in a wash tub to twenty people crowded in a slightly larger vessel, trying to paddle in unison without falling into the water.

The Legend of Cold Lake

Before settlers arrived, the Natives of the land often camped on the shores of Cold Lake. One night, a Wood Cree brave set out across the lake to visit his betrothed. Paddling swiftly and surely, he glided silently through the water. Suddenly, near the mouth of what is now known as French Bay, a gigantic fish emerged from the depths of the lake. It opened its huge jaws and clamped onto the tiny canoe, snapping it in half. • The two pieces of the canoe were found the next day, but the young man was never seen again. For years, no member of that tribe dared to cross the lake, home of the giant "Kinosoo."

East of town is Cold Lake Provincial Park. It is on a small peninsula and has showers, electrical hook-ups, a boat launch, and many scenic hiking and cross-country skiing trails. Skits, informative talks, and bird watching hikes are scheduled throughout the summer at the amphitheatre. Set up your camp while you angle for a huge trout or one of the other twenty-one fish species that inhabit the lake. Northern pike weigh up to nine kilograms (20 pounds); lake trout 4.5 to 6.8 kilograms (10 to 15 pounds); walleye to 5.4 kilograms (12 pounds).

In 1809, two fur traders travelled to near present-day Vermilion from Cold Lake. In addition to their furs, they brought back some large trout they had caught in the lake. One of the trout weighed 15.9 kilograms (35 pounds).

Chapter 11
Fort Saskatchewan to Lloydminster

History plays an important role in this section of Alberta, and is celebrated through museums, artifacts, parks, attractions, and cairns.

Go west of Mundare on Highway #16 to the Ukrainian Cultural Heritage Village. In an effort to preserve and interpret the history of the early Ukrainian settlers, a group of Albertans started the village in 1971. The Alberta government purchased the enlarged settlement in 1975, and it is now one of Alberta's largest historical sites.

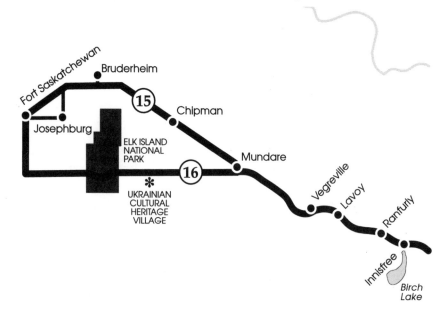

Just a few kilometres past the Ukrainian Village is Elk Island National Park, which straddles Highway #16. On the north side is a buffalo paddock, where a display herd of plains bison is kept. On the south side is an elk herd and a wood buffalo herd.

In the park across from the railway tracks in Vermillion, you will find one of the few artifacts recovered from the Frog Lake massacre. The large, black mill wheel is mounted in a row of trees on the west side of the park.

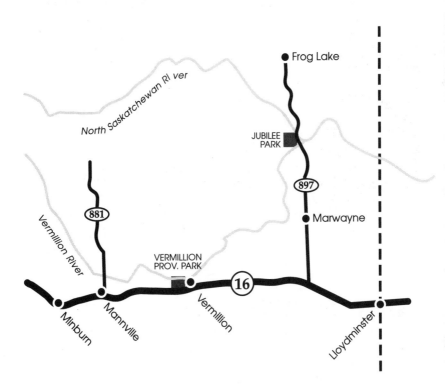

Fort Saskatchewan to Elk Island National Park

FORT SASKATCHEWAN

The posts that eventually became Fort Edmonton were first built in 1795 on the Sturgeon River, near present-day Fort Saskatchewan. Fort Augustus was built by the North West Company and Fort Edmonton by the Hudson's Bay Company. In 1802, both were transferred to where the city of Edmonton is today.

In 1875, the NWMP established their northern division at Fort Saskatchewan. They performed the first legal execution of a murderer in the district in 1879. A Cree named Katisitchen was hanged for killing and eating his family.

Fort Saskatchewan Historic Park

The main gates to the Fort Saskatchewan Historic Park are on the exact location of where the main entry way to the headquarters of G Division stood. Look for the cairn marking the position of the guard house. From the park, you can see the North Saskatchewan River, the ferry landing, and the trail from the ferry up the river bank to the community.

Many of the buildings in the 1.5 hectare (3.8 acre) park were relocated from the surrounding district or reconstructed on site. After touring the park, stop for a coffee in the Bolton schoolhouse, opened in 1905.

Since much of Fort Saskatchewan's history revolves around law enforcement, it seems fitting that the Correctional Institute is at the city limits.

That huge plant you see on the north side of Highway 15 just outside the city is the Sherritt Gordon Mines.

JOSEPHBURG AND BRUDERHEIM

Southwest of Josephburg is the Lucky Lake Trout Farm. It has been stocked with rainbow trout, so there are plenty of fish for everyone. A special dock has been built for handicapped individuals. If the fish are biting, stay overnight at the campground.

On March 4, 1960 the Bruderheim Meteorite, travelling at 2,560 kilometres (1,560 miles) per minute, struck the earth near the town. Its 300 kilogram (660 pound) weight shook homes, rattled windows, and startled people over an area of 5,478 square kilometres (2,000 square miles).

The Moravian Church in Bruderheim was constructed in 1895.

CHIPMAN

For some authentic Ukrainian food in a realistic Ukrainian setting, drive southwest to Chipman. About one kilometre before the hamlet, at the junction of Highways #15 and #834, is a large, white building about a quarter of a kilometre south of the highway. It is recognizable by the monstrous roof hanging over a short wall, the lack of windows, and the four skylights. This is the Taste of Ukraine Restaurant.

Be prepared for a surprise when you enter. The huge outside structure totally encompasses an early Ukrainian settler's home. The house is complete with a chimney, a thatched roof, and a fence around a miniature yard. You can walk entirely around the house and view it from every angle.

After your tour, dine at one of the tables in the restaurant or have a more private meal in one of the rooms of the interior house. While waiting, examine the paintings on the walls. Some are of the house before it was refinished and others are of similar old homes.

The owners brought the house from Manitoba, restored it, and constructed the restaurant around it. At the entrance is an antique bureau on which sits a decorated Ukrainian vase with flowers and a dish of hand painted Easter eggs.

The staff is very friendly and if you are wondering what to order, the pyrogies are scrumptious.

The hotel in Chipman has a veranda off its entrance, with four tables and umbrellas. On a warm day, you can sit in the shade and cool down with a cold drink. At the St. Mary's Ukrainian Greek Catholic Church in the hamlet is a monument dedicated to Wasyl Eleniak, the first Ukrainian settler to move west.

Two kilometres (1.2 miles) north is the Edmonton Soaring Club airstrip. Sailplanes are a colourful addition to the summer skies.

MUNDARE

Mundare is at the crossroads of Highways #15 and #16 and Secondary Highway #855. If you like garlic ham sausage stop in at Stawnichy's Meat Market. It is a family run business that has been in operation since 1959. Don't task for any other sausage—they only make one kind.

Go west of Mundare on Highway #16 to the Ukrainian Cultural Heritage Village. In an effort to preserve and interpret the

history of the early Ukrainian settlers, a group of Albertans started the village in 1971. The Alberta Government purchased the enlarged settlement in 1975, and it is now one of Alberta's largest historical sites.

Restored barn, Ukrainian Cultural Heritage Village

Since 1971, many old buildings have been moved onto the Ukrainian Cultural Heritage Village grounds and restored. Each structure has been fully researched, from its residents, to its construction, to historical events occurring when it was built, to the community it came from. Every room has been furnished with vintage household goods. Interpreters, dressed in period costumes, act out the lives of the former inhabitants.

Before the interpreters begin their roles, they take a three week university credit course, then study the research material that has been gathered on the building they will occupy. Many of them enjoy working here and return year after year.

Restored house, Ukrainian Village

Ukrainian Cultural Heritage Village

When you enter the grounds, you actually take a step back in time; when you converse with the interpreters, they answer as they would in the year they are portraying. If the year is 1919, the events of that year are what they discuss. • The Alberta Provincial Police constable was stationed at Andrew in 1928. He will show you his office and the cell where he keeps his prisoners. His wife will take you on a tour through their house. She explains that her husband is on twenty-four hour duty and if he wants to take their children fishing, he has to write to headquarters and ask permission to dress in civilian clothes for the day. • In another part of the village, a young Ukrainian farmer will proudly show you around his yard. He has a wagon that can be removed from its wheels and put on runners to become a sleigh, a new granary, a thatched roof barn, and a clay oven. With a strong accent, he explains how the clay oven was built and how it bakes. • Willows are piled on the platform and clay and straw, mixed together, are formed around them. When the clay is dry, the willows are burned, leaving a hollow oven. To bake bread, wood is stacked inside and set ablaze. It is replenished and maintained for about two hours, then the ashes are scraped out and the dough set inside. Fifteen loaves can be baked in about an hour.

ELK ISLAND NATIONAL PARK

Just a few kilometres past the Ukrainian Village is Elk Island National Park, which straddles Highway #16. On the north side is a buffalo paddock, where a display herd of plains bison is kept. On the south side is an elk herd and a wood buffalo herd. In the evening, watch for these large animals lying behind the fence along the highway. You may be lucky and see some new calves.

Elk Island National Park

While visiting the park, try a round at the golf course, enjoy a hike on one of the many trails, visit the interpretive centre, or take part in some of the many events scheduled over the summer. You can look through the Ukrainian Pioneer home, furnished with numerous items from pioneer days.

Motor boats are not permitted on the park's lakes, but canoes, sailboats, and rowboats are allowed on Astotin Lake. Don't try swimming; leeches are numerous in nearly all the ponds and lakes. A semi-

Buffalo at Elk Island Park

serviced campground is open from May to September and the recreation area is large enough for a football game.

Buffalo roam freely through the park so drive carefully.

At one time, large herds of elk roamed through Alberta, but by 1903 only an estimated 75 animals remained. Elk Park was established in 1906, with 20 elk and an area of 41 square kilometres (16 miles). In 1907, a herd of 716 plains buffalo was purchased by the Federal government from the Flathead Indian Reserve in Manitoba. The government shipped 400 head to Elk Park for temporary lodging, until the fence at their destination at Wainwright was completed. When they were rounded up two years later, approximately 50 bison were missed. • Elk Island was made a dominion park in 1913. The woodland was increased in 1922, with addition of 92 square kilometres (35 square miles) and it was declared a national park in 1930. Another 102 square kilometres (39 square miles) were added south of the highway in 1947, giving the park a total of 194 square kilometres (75 square miles).

Vegreville to Mannville

Vegreville is 24 kilometres (14 miles) southeast of Mundare. At one time, #16 ran through the south end of town, but now a new section of highway bypasses the town completely. Be sure to read the road signs, or you will end up in Lloydminster without ever seeing Vegreville.

Giant pysanka, Vegreville

Vegreville is famous for its Pysanka, or giant Easter egg, erected to celebrate the centennial of the RCMP and to commemorate the early Ukrainian pioneers of the area. The 9.5 metre (30 foot) high, 14,545 kilogram (32,000 pound) egg is suspended over a lovely park, with red rock paths through green grass and a footbridge over a river. The park also has a man-made pond with ducks and swans, two gazebos, and a picnic area.

A Pysanka Festival, with many displays and events exhibiting Ukrainian culture, is held on the first weekend in July. Across the railway tracks from the park is a campground for those who want to stay for the celebrations.

On the opposite side of the old highway, a little east of the Pysanka, is the Our Lady of the Highway Shrine. It is dedicated to the safekeeping of all travellers who pass through the area. The central figure is 2.25 metres (seven feet) high and was made in Italy from Carrara (Italian white) marble. This shrine is the only one of its kind in Canada.

LAVOY, RANFURLY, INNISFREE, AND MINBURN

Lavoy, Ranfurly, Innisfree, and Minburn were all bypassed when the "new" highway went through years ago. Parts of the old road are used as accesses to reach the villages. Many disused, dilapidated buildings testify to the once prosperous times of these hamlets.

Birch Lake is two kilometres (1.2 miles) south of Innisfree and Lake Wapasu is four kilometres (2.5 miles) south. You can hike or cross-country ski from the campsite at Birch Lake. At Lake Wapasu, you might want to sunbathe on the sandy beaches or swim in the blue waters. Leave your rod and tackle at home; there are no fish in either lake.

District of Alberta

Along Highway #16, just past the Innisfree access road, is the District of Alberta cairn. It reads:

In 1882, part of the North West Territories was divided into the Districts of Alberta, Assiniboia, Athabasca, and Saskatchewan. The old District of Alberta lies to the west of this cairn. In 1905, the Provinces of Alberta and Saskatchewan were created, incorporating most of the lands of the four districts.

MANNVILLE

Mannville, because of its location at the corner of Highway #881 and old Highway #16, has managed to survive better than the other nearby towns. A park and campsite are north of the railway tracks. An archway in the park is inscribed "Early Pioneer's Arch of Triumph." At the west end is an 88 mm anti aircraft gun donated by the Royal Canadian Legion Mannville No. 33 as a centennial project.

The library is in an old, red brick building on a corner of main street. Beside the library is a small, white building, with flowers planted in front and the sign "Ladies' Restroom" over the door. Stuffed chairs await tired shoppers in an anteroom, and you can freshen up in the washroom. At one time, you could read while you relaxed, but the library grew too large for the back room and had to be moved next door. The Ladies' Restroom is sponsored by the Women's Institute of Mannville.

Vermilion to Lloydminster

VERMILION

In the park across from the railway tracks in Vermilion, you will find one of the few artifacts recovered from the Frog Lake Massacre. The large, black mill wheel is mounted in a row of trees on the west side of the park.

Frog Lake

About 55 kilometres (34 miles) north of Highway #16 on Highway #897 (north of Kitscoty) is Frog Lake. The Frog Lake Massacre monument is two kilometres east of the store on the south side of the road. There is a small parking area and the site is enclosed by a fence. Inside the fence are the markers for the graves of some of the men killed in 1885. On the monument, the plaque reads:

Here on April 2, 1885, rebel Indians under Big Bear massacred Rev. Father Leon Adelard Fafard, O.M.I., Rev. Father Felix Marchand, O.M.I., Indian Agent Thomas Quinn, Farm Instructor John Delaney, John Alexander Gowanlock, William Campbell Gilchrist, George Dill, Charles Gouin, and John Williscroft. (The unrest had been caused by the Indians' near starvation, not being given

Graves at Frog Lake

any food or supplies after an extremely hard winter.) The rebellion in other areas encouraged the uprising. They took prisoners: Mrs. Theresa Delaney and Mrs. Theresa Gowanlock

• Square, wooden pedestals with drawings and descriptions of some of the communities and people involved are lined against the trees on the east edge of the graveyard.

Vermilion Provincial Park is in the northwest corner of town. When a bridge was put in over the Vermilion River, part of the river was dammed to form a lake. The provincial park is on its shores. At the entrance stands the old Vermilion train station and a caboose. Spend some time enjoying the picnic areas, beautiful scenery, and good fishing. The Vermilion School of Agriculture, now Lakeland College, was established in 1913. With campuses in both Alberta and Saskatchewan, it is Canada's first inter-provincial college. Vermilion has the largest and most modern fire fighter training school in Canada and more than 1,300 students attend courses here each year.

MARWAYNE

Travel east on Highway #16 to Kitscoty, then turn north on #897 to Marwayne, the location of the first all-cement grain elevator constructed in Canada.

For those who like rodeos, Jubilee Park (some may remember this as Lea Park), about 15 kilometres (nine miles) north of Marwayne, is famous for its June rodeo. Although the name was changed in 1982, the stampede is still billed as the Lea Park Rodeo. There is a large campground, a golf course,

Marwayne Grain Elevator

dumping station, and a mini museum displaying antique farm machinery at the park.

The Rat Fight

On Highway #16, just a few kilometres east of the road to Blackfoot, is a large sign about Alberta's rat control program. It reads:

The barn rat, or Norway rat, has long been a source of worry and concern to farmers on the Canadian prairies. Introduced to north America by sailing vessels as early as 1775, Norway rats steadily spread across the continent in the wake of advancing settlement. Reproducing prolifically, rats are responsible for eating and contaminating crops and foods, transmitting diseases, causing structural damage to homes and farm buildings, and occasionally attacking people. Rats have earned international recognition as the most destructive vertebrate animal in both economic and human health terms. • The first recorded rat colony in Alberta was discovered in 1950 on a farm in southern Alberta along Saskatchewan border. By the fall of 1951, many more rat infestations were reported along Alberta's eastern border. In 1954, the Alberta Department of Agriculture initiated a comprehensive rat control program in an eighteen mile wide control zone along the Saskatchewan border from Montana to Cold lake, to prevent the westward migration of rats into the province. The program emphasized eliminating potential harborages, ratproofing farm buildings, keeping rat bait out at all times and physically removing rat infestations. The combination of municipal Pest Control Inspectors implementing public education and effective rat eradication measures with excellent landowner cooperation contributes to the program's success. The Province of Alberta remains one of the few areas in the world that can claim a "rat free" environment.

LLOYDMINSTER

When you drive into Lloydminster, you are entering the only city in Canada spanning the border of two provinces. When you cross 50th Avenue, you enter Saskatchewan.

While in the city, camp a day or two at Weaver Park, situated on Highway #16 on the Saskatchewan side of the city. Let your children play in the tot lot or at the playground. Older children may want to spend their time at the mini golf course while you tour the sights.

Barr Colonists' Church, Lloydminster

When you enter the original church of the Barr Colonists, you step out of the sunshine into a wire cage which prevents you from wandering through the church. You are only able to stand

and look. If you want to wander, go to the Barr Colonists Museum, with its immense display of historical artifacts.

The Imhoff Art Gallery exhibits the paintings of Count Berthold Von Imhoff, an early 1900s artist from St. Walburg. Fuch's Wildlife Display features stuffed wildlife in realistic settings.

The land around Lloydminster is dotted with oil pumps and holding tanks. Husky Oil's Canadian operation began at Lloydminster in 1946, and the oil refinery is on the north west end of the city. There is a cairn in Weaver Park commemorating the gas and oil discoveries of the district.

City on a Border

In 1903, Reverend Isaac Barr founded the Barr Colonists movement. Two thousand immigrants from various English classes followed him to Canada, hoping for a better life. Rev. Barr left the colonists at Saskatoon amid accusations of fraud, and Rev. Lloyd replaced him. • Some of the colonists established homes from Battleford to Vermilion, but most of them homesteaded where Lloydminster is today. They named their headquarters after Rev. Lloyd. The settlers had to adjust to the climate and terrain of Alberta, but they had the advantage over other immigrants of already speaking English. • The Alberta/Saskatchewan border was determined in 1905 and it ran down the middle of colony. In 1930, an order of council from both provinces united the Town of Lloydminster, Saskatchewan, and the Village of Lloydminster, Alberta, into the city of Lloydminster.

Elk Island Provincial Park.

Index

F

Fabyan 21
Fairview 74
Fairview College 74
Falher 68
Father Albert Lacombe 56–57
Faust 65
Fedorah 95
Footner Lakes Forest Region 88
Forest Technology School 44
Forestburg 13
Forestburg Collieries 14
Forestry Museum 44
Fort Assiniboine 53–54
Fort Augustus 128
Fort Chipewyan 88, 110–111
Fort Edmonton 128
Fort Ethier 28
Fort George 120
Fort McKay 110
Fort McMurray 108–110
Fort Normandeau 31
Fort Ostell Museum 28
Fort Saskatchewan 128
Fort Smith 91
Fort Vermilion 88-89
Fox Creek 60-61
Frog Lake 134

G

Galloway Museum 43
Garner Lake Provincial Park 117
Ghost Lake 98
Gibbons 94
Girouxville 68
Glendon 118
Goose Mountain Ecological Reserve 52
Grand Centre 123
Grande Cache 48–49
Grande Cache Lake 49
Grande Prairie 78-79
Grandin House 57
Great Chief Park 30
Great Pumpkin Festival 33–34
Gregoire Lake Provincial Park 108
Grimshaw 84
Grizzly Ridge 65
Grouard 66

H

Hardisty 12
Hay Lakes 16-17
Hay River 90
Hell's Gate 49

Henry Wise Wood 34
Heritage Park 115
Heritage Ranch 31
High Level 87–88
High Prairie 66–67
Hines Creek 74
Hinton 44
Holden 20
Hoselaw 121
Hotchkiss 86
House River 107
Huckleberry Tower 49
Hylo 105
Hythe 81

I • J

Imhoff Art Gallery 136
Indian Cabins 90
Innisfail 32
Innisfree 132
Iron Creek Meteorite 12
Island Lake 98
Isogun Lake 60
J. Howard Pew Industrial Garden 115
Jerry Lake 60
Jessie Lake 121–122
John Wayne's Convenience Store 33
Josephburg 128
Jubilee Park 134-135

K • L

Keg River 87
Kehewin Lake 121
Kikino Métis settlement 105
Killam 12
Kimiwan Lake 67
Kinosoo Beach and Playground 124
Kinosoo Trail 124
Kinsella 21
Kinuso 65
Kleskun Hills 79
Klondike Trail 54
Koroluk Slide 22
Krause Lake Snowmobile Area 53
La Biche River 105
Lac Canard 119
Lac La Biche 104-105
Lac La Biche Inn 104
Lac La Biche Mission 105-106
Lac Ste. Anne 58
Lacombe 29-30
Lake Athabasca 111
Lake Eden 40
Lake Wabamun 40–41
Lake Wapasu 132-133

Further Reading

Breuer, Michael. *Historic Alberta*. Don Mills: Oxford, 1986.

Broadfoot, Barry. *Pioneer Years*. Toronto: Doubleday, 1976.

Brown, Craig, Ed. *The Illustrated History of Canada*. Toronto: Lester and Orpen Dennys, 1987.

Callwood, June. *Portrait of Canada*. New York: Doubleday, 1981.

The Canadian Encyclopedia. Edmonton: Hurtig, 1988.

Chalmer, Ernest. *Royal North-West Mounted Police*. Toronto: Coles, 1972.

Chatenay, Henri. *The Country Doctors*. Red Deer: Mattrix, 1980.

Colley, Kate Brighty. *While Rivers Flow*. Saskatoon: Western Producer Prairie, 1970.

Conway, J. *The West*. Toronto: Lorimer, 1983.

Dempsey, Hugh. *The Best From Alberta*. Saskatoon: Western Producer Prairie, 1981.

—, ed. *The Best of Alberta History*. Saskatoon: Western Producer Prairie, 1981.

Fryer, Harold. *Alberta — The Pioneer Years*. Langley: Stagecoach, 1979.

—. *Ghost Towns of Alberta*. Langley: Mr. Paperback, 1981.

Hamilton, Jacques. *Our Alberta Heritage*. Calgary: Calgary Power, 1978.

Hardy, W.G., ed. *Alberta, A Natural History*. Edmonton: Hurtig, 1977.

—, ed. *The Alberta Golden Jubilee Anthology*. Toronto: McClelland and Stewart, 1955.

Helgason, Gail. *The First Albertans*. Edmonton: Lone Pine, 1987.

Hocking, Anthony. *Alberta*. Scarborough: McGraw, 1979.

Holmgren, Eric and Patricia. *Over 2000 Place Names of Alberta*. Saskatoon: Western Producer Prairie, 1976.

Kidd, Robert. *Fort George*. Edmonton: Provincial Museum and Archives, 1970.

Lussier, A.S., ed. *Louis Riel and the Métis*. Winnipeg: Pemmican, 1983.

MacBeth, Reverend. *Making of the Canadian West*. Rexdale: Coles, 1973. Originally published in 1898.

MacDonald, Robert. *Owners of Eden*. Ballantree, 1974.

MacGregor, James. *Blankets and Beads*. Edmonton: Institute of Applied Arts, 1949.

—. *A History of Alberta*. Edmonton: Hurtig, 1977.

Meyers, Jay. *Canadian Facts and Dates*. Don Mills: Fitzhenry and Whiteside, 1985.

Morse, Eric. *Fur Trade Canoe Routes of Canada*. Ottawa: Morton, Baslaw & Co, 1968.

Newman, Peter. *Caesars of the Wilderness*. Harmondsworth: Viking, 1987.

—. *Company of Adventurers*. Harmondsworth: Viking, 1985.

Palmer, T. & H. *Peoples of Alberta*. Saskatoon: Western Producer Prairie, 1985.

Paterson, T.W. *Canadian Battles and Massacres*. Langley: Stagecoach, 1977.

Provincial Museum and Archives, Edmonton.

Robotti, P. and F. *Keys to Gracious Living*. Toronto: Prentice-Hall, 1972.

Sheppe, Walter, ed. *First Man West*. Los Angeles: U of California P, 1962.

Silverman, Elaine. *The Last Best West*. Montreal: Eden Press, 1984.

Spalding, David, ed. *A Nature Guide to Alberta*. Edmonton: Hurtig, 1980.

Time Life Books. *The Canadians*. Virginia, 1979.

Woodcock, George. *The Canadians*. Don Mills: Fitzhenry & Whiteside, 1979.

About the Author

Joan Donaldson-Yarmey, born in Vancouver, B.C. and raised in Edmonton, Alberta, began her career as a travel writer after her two children and her three step-children had grown up. She has written and published many travel and historical articles, complete with photographs. Three years of travel, research and writing went into the making of this book.

OTHER LONE PINE BOOKS FOR ALBERTA INCLUDE

ALBERTA TRIVIA *(REVISED)*
Don Blake

This collection of trivial and not-so-trivial information about Alberta contains hundreds of surprising and entertaining facts. A great book for long car rides and rainy-day afternoons.

ISBN 1-55105-026-9   96 pp.   8 1/2 x 11 $9.95

ALBERTA WILDLIFE VIEWING GUIDE

Each description of over fifty of Alberta's finest wildlife viewing sites is accompanied by information about available facilities, driving directions and an access map. Colour illustrations.

ISBN 0-919433-78-2 96 pp. 5 1/2 x 8 1/2 $7.95

BACKROADS OF SOUTHERN ALBERTA
Joan Donaldson-Yarmey

This book concentrates on the lesser-known attractions of southern Alberta, providing information on local artists, natural history, cultural sites and local history. Illustrated, maps.

ISBN 1-55105-021-8   144 pp.   5 1/2 x 8 1/2 $9.95

LONE PINE PICNIC GUIDE TO ALBERTA
Nancy Gibson and John Whittaker

A unique, entertaining guide to picnic spots throughout the province, with information on local history and things to see and do for each location, as well as interesting picnic menus and recipes. Illustrated, maps.

ISBN 0-919433-60-X   288 pp.   5 1/2 x 8 1/2 $11.95

NATURE ALBERTA
James Kavanagh

A handy field guide to the common flora and fauna of Alberta, it identifies 351 species of trees, plants, fish, reptiles, birds and mammals. Illustrated, range maps.

ISBN 0-919433-91-X   180 pp.   5 1/2 x 8 1/2 $14.95

Look for these books at your local bookstore, or order direct from
Lone Pine Publishing, 206, 10426 - 81 Avenue, Edmonton, Alberta T6C 1X5
Phone: (403) 433-9333   Fax: (403) 433-9646